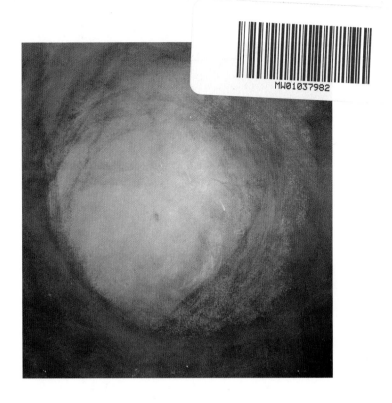

# Exploratory Surgery
## of the Soul

## *A Journey to Self Mastery*

*"Your vision will become clear only when you can look into your own heart. Who looks outside, dreams; who looks inside awakens."*

CARL JUNG

# Exploratory Surgery
## of the Soul

## *A Journey to Self Mastery*

## PEGGY FARMER, Ph.D.

SELF MASTERY INTERNATIONAL
TRYON, NORTH CAROLINA

# Exploratory Surgery of the Soul

## A Journey to Self Mastery

Although the author, editor and publisher have exhaustively
researched all sources to ensure the accuracy and completeness of
the information contained in this book, we assume no responsibility for errors, inaccuracies, omissions or any inconsistency here-
in. Any slights of people or organizations are purely unintention-
al. The women featured in Section II of this book have been given
different names to remain anonymous. Readers should use their
own judgment and inner discernment or consult a holistic medical
expert or their personal physician for specific applications to their
individual problems.

Three paintings by the late Mikaloujus Konstantinas Ciurlionis are
found on the book cover, "Creation of the World," the cover page
for Section II, "Virgo," and Section III, "The Fairy Tale of Kings."
The collected works of M.K. Ciurlionis are housed in the Kaunas
M.K. Ciurlionis Picture Gallery in Kaunas, Lithuania.
Original illustrations are by Judy Fallon of Marketing by Design
in Tarpon Springs, Florida.

ISBN 0-9705424-0-2

**Attention organizations, healing centers and schools of
spiritual/psychological development:**
Quantity discounts are available for bulk purchase of this book
for educational purposes or fund raising. Special books or book
excerpts can also be created to fit specific needs.
For more information, please contact
Self Mastery International,
373 Landrum Rd., Tryon, North Carolina 28782
or phone/fax (828) 863-4681.
**Visit our website at www.selfmasteryintl.com
for additional information.**

# Dedication

*This book is dedicated to everyone, as the journey to self mastery is a universal one involving each and every one of us. As each of us heals, the whole of the Earth heals. I honor and acknowledge all the wisdom I have received from countless sources around the world and mostly from Heaven above. I thank God for unconditional love, endless encouragement and tireless tutelage. I am thankful for the strength, power and wisdom of many other divine beings who are working so diligently to uplift this glorious planet.*

*I would also like to dedicate this book to my beloved divine mate and heavenly husband, Hector, who is the wind beneath my wings! Words cannot begin to capture the profound love I feel for you.*

*I want to express my heartfelt gratitude to the editor of this book, Jennifer Lugo, whose tireless efforts and commitment to excellence have resulted in a readable book. Many eyes proofread this text; two special "laser beams" are my sister Jennifer and especially my mother Ginny. Thank you for your literary expertise and unconditional love. I would like to express my love, adoration and admiration for my siblings Katy, Paul, Jim, Jeff and Jen. You have each shaped me into the person I am and together we have made Dad proud of us all. Many thanks and deep appreciation for the book's graphic designer, typesetter and talented illustrator, Judy Fallon.*

*I would like to thank the marvelous women and men who have shared their lives with me, who have cried with me and opened their souls to me so that this book can touch our souls and inspire the best in each of us. My heartfelt thanks go out to the countless women I've had the pleasure of working with through women's wellness retreats and seminars. I would also like to thank Dr. Letitia Ballance who has accompanied me on several retreats and has become a close friend and trusted companion on the path of self mastery. Each of you has added your melody to my life and together we've created a symphony that the whole world can enjoy. I feel honored to share in the sacred work of our transformation. I would also like to thank the lovely Joan Rogers for sharing her story along with the marvelous artwork of Mikaloujus Konstantinas Čiurlionis, a Lithuanian artist whose paintings adorn the cover and are featured in the book. Lastly, I would like to thank my wonderful colleagues at Self Mastery International, namely Malcolm Piers-Taylor, who for over ten years has been a great source of support, laughter and friendship. To all the special people in my life that I have not mentioned, please know you are loved and valued in all ways.*

*My highest wish is that each person who reads this book discovers the joy of self-love and spreads it out to each and every life they touch.*

# Contents

# Introduction

*W*e are all on a journey. Some journey into outer space to explore the vastness of the universe, others journey into the oceans to seek buried treasures, and still others journey to leave a legacy of hope through their life's work. Yet a rare few of us journey within to find the greatest gift of all...the untapped potential of our own souls.

The purpose of this book is the purpose of my life: to aid people on their journey to self-love. This exploration will bring you to the shore of your soul, assisting you to navigate a course of inner excellence, discovering the lost treasure of self mastery. Self masters are people who, above all else, have love in their hearts, optimistic thoughts in their minds, a purpose to their lives, and respect and love for themselves as well as others.

Picture self mastery as a four-rayed star. At the center is love, without which nothing could be. The star's four brightest rays symbolize mind, body, spirit and service, the guiding lights of self mastery.

The first section of this book explores the foundation of self mastery and deepens our understanding of self. The rays illuminate our inner world, shining the laser of light and love on limiting core beliefs that keep us from our brilliance. This exploratory soul searching attunes us to the language of our own soul.

The second section, Stories that Light the Way, contains inspirational life stories of women on the journey to self-love and self mastery. After enduring everything from repeated rape to echoing loneliness, these women decided to take their power back. So can you.

The book's final section, Tools for Self-Transformation, is full of tangible activities to aid your own journey to self-love. It includes guided meditations, rituals to keep you in balance, ideas for journaling, wellness tips and more.

Attaining self mastery will be easier for some, more challenging for others. For everyone, however, it's a twisting, complex journey through our elusive selves, an exploratory surgery of the soul.

# Section I

# The Four Pointed Star
# LOVE, THE CENTER

*"Give all to Love; Obey thy Heart."*

RALPH WALDO EMERSON

CHAPTER 1

# Self-Love, the Heart of Self Mastery

*T*he crux of self mastery, the center of its star, is self-love. Self-love is an inner knowing and self-confidence not affected by what other people think, say or do. It is a deep sense of self-respect. To love yourself – body, mind and spirit – is to be liberated from the ocean of opinions swirling around you. Self-love allows for a sense of equanimity in life, and the ability to rise above defamation *and* praise.

Self-love is life's finest and most fundamental tool, yet one of the most arduous to master. In our culture of competition, criticism and condemnation, we tend to downplay compliments and accomplishments, yet a single criticism upsets us for days. The reason is deceptively simple: a lack of self-love. In the absence of self-love, problems are magnified, views are distorted and your belief in yourself is seriously compromised.

*"It's only a thought, and a thought can be changed."*

LOUISE HAY

Perhaps you were deluged with negative comments and programmed to believe them as a child. Examples of negative programming might be "you stupid idiot," "you're so careless," "you can't do that," "sissy," "coward," "children should be seen and not heard," or "who do you think you are?" Such constant demeaning, painful programming hinders self-esteem and can cripple your potential.

I've worked with countless women and men, beginning with myself, to overcome devastating negative programming. Together we've witnessed the incredible healing power of positive reprogramming statements. Profound in their application, positive re-programming statements catapult self-esteem to new heights, which leads to self-love – your soul's highest state.

## The Thought Process

Re-programming a negative thought and reinforcing a positive one is easy; it simply requires attention and a deep desire to transform your life for the better. First, let's explore the anatomy of consciousness. The thinking process employs three main functions: the mind, the intellect and the subconscious. Each has a unique function. The mind takes in information through the senses (hears sounds, senses room temperature, smells, etc.); the intellect takes in information from the mind and processes it much like a computer analyzes data by making judgments, assumptions and discriminations. The subconscious takes each thought and experience and records it, creating something like a huge archival storage area. Then, these stored impressions bubble up as thoughts to the mind to be recycled over and over again. The system works like a continual biofeedback loop – there is sensory input, the intellect processes the information and impressions are stored in the subconscious. It's important to understand this process, because to attain self-love you must become an active participant in your own consciousness.

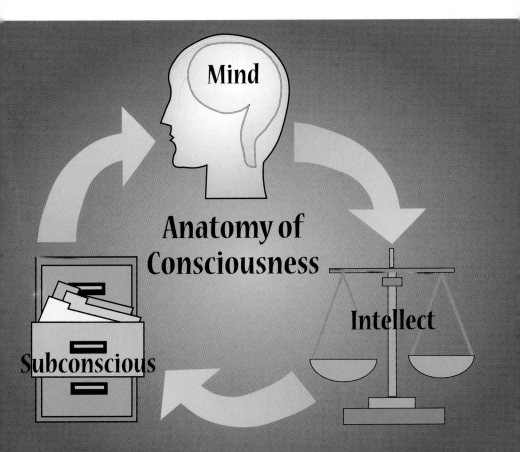

Mind

Anatomy of
Consciousness

Intellect

Subconscious

Re-directing your thoughts is like driving a car; if something runs in front of you, you immediately hit the brakes to avoid an accident. To avoid "accidents of consciousness," simply slam on the brake of your intellect to re-program a thought from self-recrimination and self-loathing to one of self-love and self-respect.

If you have a negative thought such as "there's no way I'm going to complete this project on time, I'll never finish it," use your intellect to examine that thought. Retrieve data to prove you've accomplished much in your life and are quite able to complete tasks on schedule. By doing this simple exercise you re-program your thoughts from self-effacing to self-affirming. If you let that same thought remain without the intervention of positive re-programming, you are reinforcing a mistaken belief that you can't accomplish anything. The negative thought is stored in your subconscious, again, only to sneak back into your mind any time you tackle a new project.

When you use the anatomy of consciousness to your advantage, you become like a skilled computer programmer. You quickly assess "viruses" (negative thoughts) and de-bug your thinking to eliminate the negative thoughts and create a data bank filled with positive, affirming statements. The result: an efficient, skillful mind and a sweet state of self-love.

**Self Talk**

Self talk is a powerful tool for transformation; if used to your advantage, it can be life altering. It is the essence of positive re-programming statements. We talk to ourselves the entire day whether we are aware of it or not. This non-stop chatter has a huge influence on your sense of self – so make it good.

Don't get trapped in stressful sorts of negative self talk tangents like these:

- I must have the love and approval of everyone, all the time.
- I must be perfect and competent in everything I do.
- People should act the way I think they should act.
- Things should happen when I want them to happen.
- I need a perfect love and a perfect mate to be happy.
- When people disapprove of me, it means I am bad or wrong.
- My worth as a person depends upon how much I achieve and produce or how much money I make.

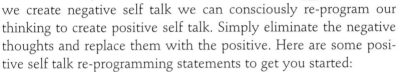

- My way of looking at the world is the only way of looking at the world.
- I hate myself.
- I am not enough or I don't do enough.
- I am too fat, ugly, tall, short, thin, sick, etc.

These limiting thoughts are stressful and alienating. Examine them to see if they are keeping you from joyful self-expression. Then, apply the antidote – positive self talk. Just as we create negative self talk we can consciously re-program our thinking to create positive self talk. Simply eliminate the negative thoughts and replace them with the positive. Here are some positive self talk re-programming statements to get you started:

- I am the creator of my own reality.
- I allow everyone to be who they are.
- I am worthy of the respect of others.
- I am strong, vibrant and healthy.
- I am beautiful and attractive in my own right.
- I love myself unconditionally.
- I enjoy moving my body and appreciate its many abilities.
- I embrace my unique body type and celebrate it.
- I am the embodiment of wellness.
- My body, mind and spirit function at an optimal level.
- My value is defined by my inner integrity, not by others.
- I honor the opinions of others and celebrate the differences.

Passionately voice these positive re-programming statements each day; the more you believe them the better they work. The better it gets, the better it gets! Use the power of your mind to assist in your transformation and allow yourself to experience the truth of these heartfelt words. If some of these affirmations are difficult to swallow at the outset, "fake it till you make it." Belief becomes biology (see chapter 15). Allow yourself to celebrate your strengths and inner beauty – when you do, you'll have a positive effect on yourself and those around you.

The greatest gift we can give our families, the world and ourselves is self-love via soulful self mastery. This chapter and the rest of this book are dedicated to transforming your beliefs from self-effacing to self-affirming, and empowering you with practical tools to assist you on the path to self-love and self mastery. Your responsibility and greatest lesson on this journey to self-love is to realize that *you alone* are responsible for your feelings of love, self-worth and fulfillment.

## Exploratory Questions for The Journey to Self Love

1. Do I love myself unconditionally?
2. Am I employing the mind as my friend or foe?
3. In what ways can you see yourself applying the "anatomy of consciousness" to change self-defeating thoughts to self-affirming thoughts?
4. Write down the top five qualities you feel you possess and ask yourself if they are being utilized in everyday life.
5. Are you willing to become an active participant on the journey to self-love?
6. What steps will you take from this day forward to achieve a greater sense of self-love?

CHAPTER 2

# Love, The Ultimate Reality

*W*ebster's dictionary defines love as "an intense affection for another person based on personal or familial ties" and "an intense attraction to another person based mainly on sexual desire." Webster goes on to list more than 20 definitions of love; let us expand our view and explore its other facets.

Just as a diamond is multifaceted and judged by the quality of its cut, clarity, carat, and color, we can ascertain the value of love that we give and receive. Is your love a cut above the rest? Can you see through the haze of limited thinking and ego to discover the real brilliance of a person or situation? Are you able to chip away the armoring and defense mechanisms that may keep you walled off from your true feelings and keep you from loving fully?

A diamond's clarity symbolizes its flawlessness and clearness. Do you have the clarity of an exquisite diamond that sparkles with truth? Is there clarity in your mind or is it cluttered with multiple agendas rather than multiple facets? Do you clearly share your true feelings with clarity and sincerity?

*"There must be the generating force of love behind every effort that is to be successful."*

HENRY DAVID THOREAU

Are you creating a colorful, multi-faceted relationship with your inner self and allowing all the shimmering parts of your iridescent core to shine through? Or, are you allowing outside influences to dull your radiance and weigh you down thereby lessening your carat weight? Self-love allows you to prevent scratches to your resilient surface and keeps sharp comments from chipping away at your self-esteem.

True love comes from within and is constant regardless of external conditions. Love is a profound healer, teacher and solvent. It washes away the past and creates space for the future.

*"There will come a time when, after harnessing the winds, the tides, and gravitation, we shall harness for God the power of love. And on that day, for the second time in the history of the world, we shall have discovered fire."*

PIERRE TEILHARD
DE CHARDIN

Unconditional love allows you to accept each and every part of yourself and others with compassion and gentleness. Yet it also holds you accountable to higher standards and spurs you on to continued growth and evolution. Love is the ability to open your heart and allow all facets of your inner diamond to be shared with the world. The most powerful force in the universe is love. Love and God are synonymous. Love is the bridge between past, present and future. Love is the element that keeps all things in context. Love is the fuel of the universe, the food of our souls, the nourishment for our body, mind and spirit. It is welcomed everywhere and is truly priceless. Love grows exponentially with continued use. Love can stop wars, end hunger, heal the sick, mend the mind, soothe the soul, remove the pain – love can move mountains. Love is limitless in its application to every aspect of our lives. Without love, we are lost. We need to be loved, we need to give love, and we need to receive love to fully flourish and grow. The love I speak of is without judgment and expectations – it is a divine love that is unconditional and from the heart.

How do we love like that? Ask yourself, "Do I love myself unconditionally?" We can't possibly love others unconditionally if we don't love ourselves unconditionally. When we say we "love" another, we have to ask ourselves if we are acting from a space of love or motivated by ego or other ulterior motives such as seeking love in order to get love in return. If we employ the power of love in each of our tasks, no matter how mundane, success is guaranteed. Love is the ultimate reality!

# *Exploratory Questions for Love, the Ultimate Reality*

1. Do I love all aspects of myself and embrace them into wholeness?
2. Am I my greatest advocate?
3. Do I question my abilities and allow self-doubt to keep me from my brilliance?
4. Am I impatient with myself and think I don't do enough?
5. To whom am I comparing myself? Is the comparison reasonable?
6. Am I honoring my unique talents and gifts?
7. Am I using them for the highest and best good for the planet and myself?

## *Elixir of Love*

**Directions for Use:**

Love is to be lavishly lathered onto every being with whom you come in contact.

Openly share this Elixir with others and watch alchemy in action.

Volunteer to voluminously spread this Elixir everywhere you go.

Endeavor to make each day an outpouring of Love and watch it bubble into the waters of life, washing away all doubt, fear and separation.

♥ Our task is to fill ourselves to overflowing with this exquisite elixir and then radiate it out into the world in the purest state of unconditional love possible.

17

While traveling in England, I came upon this profound document about love.

# The Cathar Prophecy of 1244 A.D.

*The Church of Love*

*It has no fabric, only understanding.*

*It has no membership save those who know they belong.*

*It has no rivals because it is non-competitive.*

*It has no ambition, it only seeks to serve.*

*It knows no boundaries for nationalisms are unloving.*

*It is not of itself because it seeks to enrich all groups and religions.*

*It acknowledges all great Teachers of all the ages who have shown the truth of Love.*

*Those who participate, practice the Truth of Love in all their beings.*

*There is no walk of life or nationality that is the barrier.*

*Those who are, know.*

*It seeks not to teach but to be and by being, enrich.*

*It recognizes that the way we are may be the way of those around us, because we are the way.*

*It recognizes the whole planet as a Being of which we are a part.*

*It recognizes that the time has come for the supreme transmutation, the ultimate alchemical act of conscious change of the ego into a voluntary return to the whole.*

*It does not proclaim itself with a loud voice, but in the subtle realms of loving.*

*It salutes all those in the past, who have blazed the path but have paid the price.*

*It admits no hierarchy nor structure, for no one is greater than another.*

*Its members shall know each other by their deeds and being and by their eyes and by no other outward sign save the fraternal embrace.*

*Each one will dedicate their life to this silent loving of their neighbor and environment and the planet, while carrying out their task, however humble or exalted.*

*It recognizes the supremacy of the great idea which may only be accomplished if the human race practices the supremacy of Love.*

*It has no reward to offer, either here or in the hereafter, save that of the ineffable joy of being and loving.*

*Each shall seek to advance the cause of understanding, doing good by stealth and teaching only by example.*

*They shall heal their neighbor, their community, and our Planet.*

*They shall know no fear and feel no shame and their witness shall prevail over all odds.*

*It has no secret, no arcanum, no initiation, save that of true understanding of the power of Love and that, if we want it to be so, the world will change, but only if we change ourselves first.*

*All those who belong, belong;*

*They belong to the CHURCH OF LOVE.*

# CHAPTER 3

# Compassionate Communication

Compassionate communication is essential to healthy human interactions. It is vital to our emotional well-being and our very existence. We communicate with each other via our words, our emotions, our facial expressions and our actions. The subject of compassionate communication has a great deal to do with self-love, because often our inability to communicate effectively stems from low self-esteem. We know that low self-esteem is directly related to a lack of self-love. Assertive communication requires that you assert yourself, speaking your truth with confidence and self-respect. The more you stand up for yourself and act in a manner that you respect, the higher your self-esteem will be.

*"Man must evolve for all human conflict a method which rejects revenge, aggression and retaliation. The foundation of such a method is love."*

MARTIN LUTHER KING, JR.

A common thread of uneasiness in business and family life is a lack of compassionate, effective communication. Breakdowns in communication wreak untold havoc in organizations and families. Why? Because the majority of people have never been formally schooled in the fine art of compassionate, assertive communication.

We will be exploring four communication styles that we employ consciously and unconsciously in our daily lives. The four main types are passive, aggressive, passive aggressive and assertive. (See Figure 1 for more details).

Many of the communication styles we've learned are unhealthy. Each of us filters the world through our own lens of past experiences, so we often use communication styles modeled by our parents or primary caregivers. We may be passive and avoid conflict because we learned that to do anything less would result in bodily harm. Do you allow yourself to be pushed around, can't speak up in meetings, or find yourself saying, "I'm sorry" for things you didn't do? Passive communicators tend to appear weak and self-conscious. Deep down they feel insecure and may experience self-doubt. Being passive perpetuates the cycle of negative thinking and self-esteem drops even lower. Furthermore, passivity in the workplace results in unspoken expectations and affects both you and your colleagues because they sense you want to say more but won't.

Conversely, aggressive and dominating personalities tend to come on too strong. Because of their life experiences, they are full of hurt, anger, and resentment and may lash out at others or overly defend issues. This aggressive response tends to evoke aggression in others and make the aggressive communicator even more out of control, which alienates him further from friends or colleagues.

Passive aggressive communicators will say one thing to your face and another thing behind your back. Passive aggressive communication is the most insidious of all the communication styles because it is harder to confront and subtler than the aggressive or passive communicator; in fact, in the workplace, it is the most common communicative disorder. The result is a backbiting environment where trust is non-existent and people feed into negativity and gossip. Passive aggressive communicators act in this way to achieve a pseudo sense of control. They feel that if they can subtly defame another team player, they are somehow achieving a victory for themselves. This strategy stems from a culture steeped in competition. Few of us have learned to be assertive and communicate with compassion.

The gold standard of compassionate communication lies in the ability to be assertive. People often misunderstand the definition of assertive and tend to think of assertive people as aggressive. Part of the reason for that misconception is people often think they are communicating assertively when they are actually being aggressive. Hence, the confusion and anxiety invoked when people think they have to learn to be assertive communicators. Assertive communicators should always be compassionate in their delivery. Assertive communication is the ability to relay a clear message, without blame or criticism. Compassionate listening requires a level of deep connection beyond mere attention to the speaker's words. It allows

FIGURE 1

| Communication Styles | Verbal | Non Verbal |
|---|---|---|
| **Passive** | Apologetic words (I'm sorry) <br> Failure to come to the point <br> Rambling, disconnected <br> Self-defeating | Actions instead of words, hoping someone will guess the meaning or ask what you want ("sigh" language) <br> Appear insecure <br> Nervous gestures <br> Voice is weak, hesitant, soft and sometimes wavering <br> Eyes are averted, downcast or teary <br> Usually lean for support or stance is stooped, excessive head nodding <br> Hands are fluttery and often clammy |
| **Aggressive** | Loaded words <br> Accusations <br> Subjective "You" messages that blame <br> Puts others down <br> Dictator | Exaggerated show of strength <br> Flippant, sarcastic style <br> Air of superiority <br> Controlling <br> Voice tends to be loud, tense, shrill, shaking and demanding <br> Eyes are cold, expressionless, narrowed; as though staring right through you but not "seeing" you <br> Hands on hip, feet apart, body is stiff and unyielding <br> Hands are clenched, abrupt gestures; finger pointing and fist pounding |
| **Passive Aggressive** | Shifts responsibility to others <br> Talks about others behind their back <br> Manipulative <br> Failure to say what they really mean | Actions appear defiant yet suspect <br> Often appear clueless <br> Voice is hesitant, wavering or overly defensive <br> Tend to avoid direct eye contact or will look to others for back-up <br> Stance appears receptive but is also resistant and shifts from side to side <br> Hands are often clammy and clenched |
| **Assertive** | Clear statement of what you want <br> Honest feelings <br> Objective words <br> "I" messages <br> Accepts responsibility of self | Attentive listener <br> Communicates with confidence, caring and strength <br> Voice is firm, warm and well-modulated <br> Eyes are open, gaze is direct and relaxed, eyes convey receptivity <br> Good eye contact throughout conversation <br> Body is well-balanced and relaxed, posture is straight and erect <br> Hands are demonstrating relaxed motions |

you to hear the sadness behind the anger, the pain behind the frustration. Attentive listening means giving someone your undivided attention. Most of us are already preparing our rebuttal long before the person we are speaking with has finished his thoughts.

Examine the four communication styles in Figure 1. Notice there is a verbal and non-verbal component. Find which one of these styles most aptly describes you. Most of our communication, whether we are aware of it or not, is non-verbal. Albert Mehrabian's studies of listening revealed that 7 percent of meaning is interpreted from words, 93 percent from voice tone and body language *(Silent Messages: Implicit Communication of Emotions and Attitudes)*. This research supports the theory of first impressions, where we size each other up and have an instantaneous reading on believability and trust. Unless a speaker is believable – congruent in voice, words and body language – the listener may make a judgment about the speaker's lack of trustworthiness. What is your body saying? Are you saying what you mean and meaning what you say? Is this the message you want to convey with your body? As a parent or educator, are you role-modeling assertive communication? If your child sees you acting with self-respect, standing up for yourself, communicating honestly, she will learn to do these things as an adult.

Communication problems in both organizations and families often stem from incongruence in thought and action. People may say one thing and mean another, and we are all well-trained to pick up intuitively on the differences. To remedy this, simply be honest with yourself. State what you want in clear terms. Be direct and concise and speak with confidence. If you find yourself getting anxious while interacting with someone, take a few deep breaths and remind yourself that no one or nothing can affect you unless you let them. It is helpful to role-play a potentially stressful scenario in your mind and practice communicating with ease and grace. Visualize yourself skillfully handling a conflict and calmly asserting your opinions without fear or anger. Remember that you have choices about how you will respond to people or events. Just because someone is irate or irrational doesn't mean you have to be. Standing in your power even when other people are not standing in theirs is a sure sign of self mastery.

It is with compassionate ears and a receptive heart that we can truly be the masterful communicators we are destined to be. It requires self-love to be a compassionate communicator and it takes courage to assert your heartfelt truths with confidence.

## *Exploratory Questions for Compassionate Communication*

1. Do I communicate with compassion or am I quick to get on the defensive and judge others?
2. What styles of communication do I employ.... am I passive, aggressive, assertive or passive aggressive? Do I shift between different types?
3. What can I do to become more assertive and clearly state what I want without feeling guilty or intimidated or angry?
4. Am I willing to practice and rehearse the fine art of assertive communication in the theatre of my own life?
5. What are my motives when I communicate with others and do I calmly handle conflict?
6. Do I take it personally if someone disagrees with me?
7. Is love the foundation of my communication and do I share this feeling with others?

CHAPTER 4

# The Art of Loving Relationships

*T*here is nothing more important in our lives than our relationships, whether with ourselves, our loved ones, family and friends or anyone who crosses our path. We all need to co-exist and co-create healthy, happy and fulfilling relationships that nurture and support us.

Our relationships help us overcome barriers, fears and insecurities. They provide reflective opportunities that mirror our own

strengths and weaknesses and serve to increase our inner knowingness. Even difficult relationships provide us with wisdom gleaned from the school of hard knocks. We have to learn to discern. Determining what is appropriate for us in relation to others can be an eye-opening experience. It takes time because we sometimes have to experience what we don't want to get clearer about what we do want. For example, some of the most dysfunctional relationships facilitate the greatest learning by showing us what is inappropriate for us; my most difficult relationships taught me some of my

*Constantin Brancusi, The Kiss*

most valuable lessons. Those relationships teach us boundaries, remind us to stand in our power, and even show us how to let go. Once learned, this wisdom will serve you well on the journey to self-love and self mastery.

In order to create loving, supportive relationships, one needs to be conscious! We need to bring our whole selves to our relationships. To be fully present in our lives, we need to not be distracted by the past or preoccupied with the future; all of these distractions prevent us from making joyful connections in the present. We must remove old blocks and remove ego to be fully present. In their groundbreaking book on relationships, *Conscious Loving,* Drs. Gay and Kathlyn Hendricks outline some key preliminary factors that assist in the process of conscious relationships. They have identified several core commitments essential to transforming co-dependency. The six co-commitments are:

## ✦ Co-commitment 1
I commit myself to being close, and I commit myself to clearing up anything in the way of my ability to do so.

## ✦ Co-commitment 2
I commit myself to my own complete development as an individual.

## ✦ Co-commitment 3
I commit to fully revealing myself in relationships, not to concealing myself.

## ✦ Co-commitment 4
I commit myself to the full empowerment of people around me.

## ✦ Co-commitment 5
I commit to acting from the awareness that I am 100 percent the source of my reality.

## ✦ Co-commitment 6
I commit myself to having a good time in my close relationships.

While some of these co-commitments may seem daunting at first, they serve as a guide to lead you to the goal of a loving, co-committed relationship. Intimacy can be easy for some and difficult for others. If we've been hurt in relationships - and let's face it, who hasn't - we may feel tentative or guarded when exploring a new relationship. However, before we dive deeply into the waters of commitment, we need to remove hidden rocks, broken dreams, shattered hearts and frosty icebergs of unexpressed emotion that prevent us from being fully open to love.

Picture your life as a clean slate, a blank chalkboard that has just been erased of any and all wrongdoing from others or yourself.

Now see yourself acting and relating with others from a fresh perspective, unencumbered by past pains. Most of us have become walking filing cabinets with our drawers stuffed full of old records that tell the tale of betrayal, loss, injustices, broken promises and failed relationships. To fully commit to conscious loving, purge the files! Let go of inner clutter and clear the decks for a new voyage into uncharted waters. Instead of waiting for others to change or grow, be the source of your own self-development. Be the source of your own power. Do not play the victim role in relationships because you are never a victim. Where you are in a relationship is where you choose to be; if you don't like it, work to change it. Remember you have choices as to whom you spend your time with. We teach people how to treat us. If you are in a difficult relationship and feel that you are not being respected or valued, respect and value yourself enough to speak your truths and set limits. No one or nothing can affect you unless you let them. Create your own reality based on what you desire to see manifest in your life.

In co-dependent relationships, one partner often dis-empowers the other to keep the dysfunction alive and to divert attention from the real issues. We may defer our growth because we feel our partner may not want to grow with us. This causes us to feel stunted, and we stagnate and become resentful. Have the courage to delve into uncomfortable issues, discuss the undiscussables and create clear communication through truth telling. Most relationships struggle because people fail to tell the microscopic truth about feelings, thoughts and actions. A lot of tension can be relieved in a relationship just by being honest and sharing your heartfelt truths, not keeping them locked inside. We must also communicate our love regularly. Dr. Leo Buscaglia conducted a survey of couples who had sustained successful, long term, loving relationships and asked what their keys to success were. More than 85 percent said the most essential quality for a lasting, loving relationship was the ability to communicate.

Co-commitment requires the ability to empower and encourage your loved ones. Empower your partner, friends and family to be the best they can be. Instead of downplaying each other's talents, celebrate your gifts. I remember a couple who had a hard time honoring and empowering each other. Both were talented in their own right; she had a beautiful voice and he had a great sense of humor. Conflict arose, however, when she was asked to sing at family gatherings and parties. While she sang, he thought she was showing off. Upon further exploration, it became clear he carried baggage about not being validated and would often downplay his talent. Like many others, he consciously understated his abilities with a pseudo sense of modesty and expected the same behavior from his partner. None of this posturing is necessary and is all related to the contortions of the mind and convoluted thinking of our ego. Love is not ego-based or fear-based; it is deeply rooted in self-love. Without that firm foundation, it's difficult to give what you don't have to others. Thousands of years ago, the Apostle Paul knew the importance of love and how to differentiate between love and the imposter.

*"If I have the gift of prophecy and can fathom all mysteries and all knowledge, and if I have a faith that can move mountains, but have not love, I am nothing. If I give all I possess to the poor and surrender my body to the flames, but have not love, I gain nothing. Love is patient, love is kind. It does not envy, it does not boast, it is not proud. It is not rude, it is not self-seeking, it is not easily angered, it keeps no record of wrongs. Love does not delight in evil but rejoices with the truth. It always protects, always trusts, always hopes, always perseveres. Love never fails. And now these three remain: faith, hope and love. But the greatest of these is love."*

PAUL, 1 CORINTHIANS 13

*T*he last co-commitment of a conscious relationship speaks of having a good time. Many couples I've worked with spend too much time hammering out the details of their relationships and little time having fun. Yes, relationships are meant to be joyful and fun-filled! If we choose to see the specialties in ourselves and our loved ones rather than being quick to find fault, happiness will result. Find fun things to do as a couple. Have a date night once a week without any outside distractions, including TV; engage in each other.

The six co-commitments help clearly articulate a deep desire to co-create a healthy, loving relationship. In healthy relationships, partners affirm that both closeness and individuality are important. In a co-committed relationship, you commit yourself to being 100 percent you in your relationships. In our couples' retreat, Adventures of the Heart, my husband and I ask each partner to share these co-commitments. In doing so they take a stand for their own evolution. In this new millennium choose to be conscious in your loving and enjoy the beauty of fulfilling, healthy, enlightened relationships.

## Exploratory Questions for the Art of Loving Relationships

1. Do I keep myself closed off from intimacy because of past pains?
2. Are my unspoken expectations preventing me from being happy in my relationships?
3. What steps am I taking to increase my emotional self-awareness?
4. Do I allow myself to express a variety of emotions by feeling sad, angry, confused, vulnerable or fearful? Do I express my joy, contentment, clarity, strength and gratitude?
5. Do I speak my truths with an open heart?
6. Am I celebrating my strengths and the strengths of those around me?
7. Am I encouraging the growth and evolution of my loved ones?
8. How do I honor others and myself?
9. Do I let others decide my state of consciousness?
10. Am I having fun with my relationships?

# THE RAY OF THE SPIRIT

*"No coward soul is mine,*
*No trembler in the world's*
*storm-troubled sphere:*
*I see Heaven's glories shine,*
*And faith shines equal,*
*arming me from fear."*
EMILY BRONTË

CHAPTER 5

# Letting Go of Fear

*F*ear is a barrier for all those on the path to self mastery and self-love. Every spiritual surgeon feels the need to excise fear from the heart, lest it choke off the flow of life and spontaneity. We let fear keep us in limitation and lack. We let fear keep us from trying because we are afraid to fail. We let fear keep us from reaching new heights because we are afraid to succeed. We don't allow ourselves to fully live because we are so afraid to die. We limit our intimacy and deep connection with others because we are afraid to be hurt. We are afraid to try new things – push the envelope so to speak – because we perceive we may lose control. One of our most limiting fears is the fear of loving fully, living wide open and being the powerful souls that we truly are. Living in fear prevents us from living in love. Living in love requires us to open our hearts and be fully responsible for the lives we are creating. The key to freedom from this fear is choosing to stop being something you are not, becoming totally clear and absolutely authentic. You no longer have any investment in suffering, you no longer have bad days, and you no longer play the victim role. When you are in this place, you are powerful beyond measure.

> *"Our doubts are traitors, and make us lose the good we oft might win by fearing to attempt."*
>
> WILLIAM SHAKESPEARE

This beautiful poem by Marianne Williamson illustrates the struggle we have with letting go of fear and living wide open.

## Let Your Light Shine

*O*ur deepest fear is not that we are inadequate;
Our deepest fear is that we are powerful beyond measure.
It is our light, not our darkness, that most frightens us.
We ask ourselves, who am I to be brilliant, gorgeous,

*talented and fabulous?*
*Actually, who are you not to be? You are a child of God.*
*Your playing small doesn't serve the world.*
*There is nothing enlightened about shrinking so that other*
*    people won't feel insecure around you. We are born to make*
*    manifest the glory of God that is within us.*
*It is not just in some of us; it is in everyone.*
*And as we let our own light shine, we unconsciously give*
*    other people permission to do the same. As we are*
*    liberated from our own fear, our presence automatically*
*    liberates others.*

How poignantly this poem exposes the paralyzing power of fear and limiting beliefs. Fear is an illusion. There is a great acronym for fear found in *Conversations with God, An Uncommon Dialogue, Book 1* by Neal Donald Walsch "...fear is false evidence appearing real." We spend half our lives worrying about things that never happen. We waste inordinate amounts of energy fearing other people, the past, the future, the IRS, the world, the stock market, the next-door neighbor and even ourselves. Many of us are afraid to experience our own feelings because we fear that if we really let our guard down and begin to live wide open, our emotions would flood us.

Behind the majority of our fears is simple anxiety and the neurotic tendency to want to control every facet of our lives. If we let go of control and let go of the belief that we need to fear everything and everyone, our world and everyone in it would breathe a sigh of relief. Instead, we keep the fear machine going by feeding into it. We stand around our offices drinking coffee and talking about the 6 o'clock news, giving our attention and precious energy to the rapes, murders, robberies and global conflicts that happened the day before. Many people have become protestors of life and cast a negative net of fear on everyone they meet. Be a proactive citizen and focus on ways to make the home, workplace and world a better place to be. If you give your attention to everything wrong with the world, where is the attention to transform it? If we complain about a problem, are we willing to do our part to correct it?

Another common fear is the fear of responsibility. We feel quite comfortable complaining about people, things, events, and the economy, but we often feel disempowered or feel that our one voice won't make a difference. We then shut down and do little or nothing at all. Responsibility doesn't have to be a scary word; it is very empowering to release your fear and become a change agent. We are architects of change whether we accept the responsibility or not. Do not let yourself become overwhelmed by a feeling of responsibility; take small steps everyday to make your life better and by doing so, you shift from helpless to hopeful and from fearful to fearless. Build a firm foundation of love and self-respect with

the mortar of self-love. What structures are you creating? Are you creating a foundation of fear or love? We can either frame the world as fear-based or love-based. A fear-based world is filled with suspicion, doubt, ulterior motives, anxiety and dread. A love-based world is filled with acceptance, faith, trust, openness, joy, peace and contentment. Which world are you fueling with your priceless energy? It takes more energy to live in fear than to live in love.

Letting go of fear does not mean you no longer have discernment or you are at the mercy of anyone. It means you use your intuition and sense the world around you. If you perceive a potentially dangerous situation, simply move away. Don't do an activity you feel may harm you. Being cautious doesn't mean being paranoid about everyone you meet, assuming people are guilty before proven innocent, or thinking people can't be trusted until they are trustworthy. That's like saying, "I'll love you unconditionally if you meet these certain conditions first."

Fear drains your energy and weakens your immune system; worse, it tends to feed on itself. The more fear you feel, the more anxious you become and the more adrenaline you secrete which taxes the nervous system further. Fear has repercussions both psychologically as well as physiologically. If you fear a job interview, you will be self-conscious, nervous and probably won't be as smooth as you'd like to be. Physically, your hands will be clammy and moist, your throat may become dry, and depending on the level of anxiety, your body may even shake.

Fear is not something to avoid or shove under the rug. Fear must be dealt with and resolved. Exploratory surgery of the soul allows us to shine a laser of truth on our fear-based beliefs and cut them away. Resolving fears requires a deep look at them. What fears are you harboring? Are you afraid of failure? If so, why? Are you afraid of success? Do you know how you developed that fear? Are you likely to avoid fear when fear rears its ugly head? Do you hope it will go away forever?

The treatment for fear is simple, but it requires dedication and courage. By looking at your fears, you can begin to decode the messages and unplug from the beliefs that hold you captive. Some of us are afraid to change so we need to purposely do things out of our comfort zone until we become comfortable with change. Some of us are afraid to speak up in front of a group so we need to heal the part of us that feels unworthy and practice speaking our truths a little at a time until we feel more at ease. Some of us are afraid to dream so we need to dream big and begin to implement those dreams one by one. Let go of fear and fully live!

## *Exploratory Questions for Letting Go of Fear*

1. What am I afraid of? (List your fears.)
2. Do I let my fears keep me from my full potential?
3. What steps am I willing to take to release self-limiting beliefs, face my fears and transform them?
4. Have I deeply explored my areas of resistance and understood my fears?
5. How would I feel if I really let my light shine and quelled my inner fears?
6. Am I willing to use my precious energy to fuel a love-based world rather than a fear-based world?

CHAPTER 6

# Letting Go of Limitations

$T$he first lesson in letting go of limitations is to acknowledge that many of them are self-imposed. You yourself are the perpetrator. To explore how we limit ourselves, we must examine our core beliefs. Core beliefs comprise our internal belief systems, made up of many different, often conflicting, messages.

What keeps us in limitation and lack? Primarily it's lingering doubts and old beliefs placed there by parents, relatives, friends, and our own selves. The process begins at birth. An endless stream of fears, hopes, anxieties, cautions, and do's and don'ts are fed to our receptive young minds that lack the infrastructure to determine if these beliefs are fear-based or love-based. As adults, we may find ourselves defending deeply held core beliefs, many of which we have never questioned or challenged. Unless we are consciously examining our behavior patterns from a fresh, empowered perspective, we may think it is normal to fight, yell, be co-dependent, dis-empowered or passive, depending on the role models we had as children. Try to pinpoint times when you learned to give your power away, accepting disappointment as normal and viewing limitation as a natural state. For example, if you grew up poor, it seemed the natural assumption that you'd be poor as an adult, but that does not have to be the case.

Many of us experienced childhood with fear, accompanied by a growing uneasiness in dealing with others and ourselves. At some point the world became a frightening place dealt with only by making internal compromises about who we really are. For example, you may have been cautioned never to talk to strangers, yet you longed to be open with others and share the delight of being a child. Or perhaps you expressed your opinion about something at home or school only to be ridiculed or berated. We somehow learned to compromise our true selves in order to keep the peace, or we adopted aggressive defense mechanisms to keep others at bay. In either case, we accepted limitation over the real beauty of our true selves. We were then stuck in a fog of limited thinking, blocking our perceptions and attitudes and replacing some of our spontaneity with what seemed "safe." We began to doubt our surroundings and ourselves. We began to silence the voice of intuition and higher knowing for fear of being chastised or made fun of. We accepted our fate that some things are just not possible. Slowly our inner wisdom was replaced with society's perception of can and can't, right and wrong.

> *"Self-reverence, self-knowledge, self-control – these three alone lead to sovereign power."*
>
> ALFRED, LORD TENNYSON

As adults, then, we take on these dysfunctional paradigms and fold them into our personalities. When we try to change and begin to consciously awaken to the potential of self-love, these changes may be unsettling to those closest to us. If you choose to quit smoking but your partner doesn't, for example, he or she may see the change as threatening.

While building a loving, co-committed relationship, setting boundaries may be unsettling. If you suddenly decide to join a gym as part of your wellness plan, and your partner doesn't want you to, tension can result. He or she may want you at home, jealous of your motivation and empowerment. The uneasiness is due to clear limits being set; your partner can no longer rely on expected outcomes. This does not usually occur on a conscious level. It's not framed as, "I am going to foster co-dependency in this relationship to maintain power over rather than power with." Because these core beliefs are much more subtle and entrenched, it is difficult to change them.

There is no blame inferred here as we are all traveling our own path. We are products of our environment but we have to take responsibility for who we are *today*. We must stand in our power and stay focused on what our true core values are. Just as quickly as we bought into the illusion of lack, we can readily embrace and affirm a new vision of abundance, limitlessness, good will and harmony.

## Letting Go

Letting go is an ever-evolving process. Part of our healing process lies in removing distorted perceptions we have about our bodies, minds and spirits. Changing behavior requires the ability to

35

look deeply at your thoughts. It's simple – think about what you are thinking about. To change your life, change your behavior. To change your behavior, change your thoughts. As you think, so you become. Focus on the thoughts that cause you to feel disempowered, and begin to remove those old beliefs that limit you. Thoughts are like seeds that germinate in the fertile soil of our subconscious and conscious minds. Monitor the quality of your mental soil and nourish it with the fertilizer of nutrient-rich thoughts. We have thousands and thousands of thoughts a day. How conscious are we of these numerous thoughts? By becoming aware of our thoughts we become the conscious creators of our own reality. When we start examining our thoughts we begin to understand the fundamental role they play in our lives. Rather than being the victims of our thoughts, we take charge of the scenarios playing in our minds. We become the victors. As we begin to check the quality of our thoughts, we begin to change the quality of our lives.

In addition to thinking about what we are thinking about, another colossal factor in letting go of limitations is beginning to identify our emotions. Emotions can flood us if we allow them and many unexpressed emotions limit our clarity. Embark on an exploratory journey of your own emotions. If you feel fear in a certain situation, ask yourself where that fear is coming from. If there is sadness, what unhealed part of you needs to be nurtured? If there is anger, why do you feel that everyone needs to agree with you? If you feel self-doubt, why do you feel the need to prove yourself worthy? This type of mental and emotional checking allows us to live deeply and profoundly in the now. We become totally authentic and honest inside and out.

It requires courage to shine the light of truth on our shadow side. To coax the darkness from within ourselves we must examine the fears, the past or anything that keeps us from our brilliance. We need to gently integrate these parts of ourselves into a state of wholeness. The result is that we will love ourselves unconditionally, and love is all there is. Remember, love is the balm that soothes the soul, mends the mind and balances the body. Look into your heart and return to innocence, return to your true self. Make the first thought of each day an uplifting one and reaffirm your strength and sense of belonging. We can change our lives by changing our thoughts, feelings and behavior. Know that what you give your attention to is what you create in your life, so choose wisely. Let each of us begin to re-program any self-defeating thoughts and simply be the powerful self masters we truly are.

There is a peace that comes with being soul-conscious, with centering ourselves in the knowingness that everything is a stepping-stone to our ultimate goal. We can choose to believe miracles happen and all things are possible. We can transmute anything that is painful into joy. The past affects us because we allow it to. Let go of limitations; make a conscious commitment to re-focus, re-direct and re-dedicate your life to being the fully conscious self master you truly are!

## Exploratory Questions for Letting Go of Limitations

1. Examine areas of your life where you have trouble letting go of control. In what ways can you let go of some areas of your life and simply go with the flow?
2. Are you letting the past keep you from succeeding in the future?
3. What unquestioned core beliefs do you hold that may be limiting you?
4. How can you let go of limited thinking and become the empowered self master that you truly are?
5. Will you become more conscious of your assets rather than your liabilities and employ the power of positive thinking to catapult you out of limitations and into limitless thinking?

37

CHAPTER 7
# Honoring the Teacher Within

*M*ost of us look outside ourselves for answers to the most pressing issues and questions in our lives. We've been trained to seek outside solutions from other sources, rather than honoring our source within. Sometimes those well-meaning sources have not assisted us in our evolution. One of the most important aspects on the journey to self-love and self mastery is honoring your teacher within. Each of us has a huge archive of wisdom and knowledge to draw upon. We simply need to listen to our intuition and trust our inner knowingness. If you don't go within, you go without. We don't need another teacher, guru or pundit to guide us on this inner journey. We need only ourselves, love and our courage to guide the way. When we take the time to go within, we begin to feel the power of our own source rather than "outsourcing." We begin to feel stronger, clearer and less cluttered by the beliefs of others. While those other voices may have your best interest at heart, no one knows your inner landscape better than you.

Tapping into the teacher within requires introspection and a deep trust in yourself. How often do you listen to your inner voice? How often do you override your inner voice if it conflicts with your teachers or organized religion or society at large? How often do you forego your gut feelings because you think they're not based in fact? How many times throughout your life have you silenced that quiet voice within, and then regretted not listening to your inner wisdom?

Let me share with you a story I found rather enlightening: A man went off to the East to see a wise sage. Upon his arrival to the guru's cave he said "I want to know about your philosophy, I want to know what you know." So the old sage picked up his teapot and poured tea in the man's cup and poured tea in his own cup. The man then said, "Old man talk to me, I want to know, I want to know about your philosophy." The old man picked up the teapot and again poured tea into the man's cup. At this point, the man became annoyed and said, "I came thousands of miles because they told me that you were the best and you had all the answers. I came to you because I want answers; I want to know what you know." And so the sage picked up the teapot and poured more tea in his cup and kept pouring the tea until it poured over the cup into the saucer and onto the table and into the man's lap. The man jumped to his feet and was furious and said, "I don't like being treated this way, what are you doing, you are telling me nothing, I want to know!" And the old sage looked him in the eyes and said, "You came with a cup full of perceived ideas, I cannot fill anything that is already filled."

*"Knowing others is wisdom;*
*Knowing the self is enlightenment*
*Mastering others requires force;*
*Mastering the self requires strength"*

LAO TSU

An exciting opportunity awaits if you drink deeply from the cup of your own wisdom. Knowingness comes from within and not from without. You will no longer feel the need to externalize your decisions, weighing the input of others for hours, weeks or months. Instead you'll quiet your mind, go within, and ask for your higher guidance to supply you with the answer. What do you want to know? What do you want to learn? To explore these questions and quiet the mind, you'll need to fine-tune your ability to *focus* and end your mind's chatter. As you practice, confidence and clarity will follow.

## Barriers to Honoring the Teacher Within

Responsibility, a daunting barrier to honoring the teacher within, can be both empowering and scary. People often seek leaders – whether it's a friend, teacher, priest or guru – and transfer their power and decision-making capabilities over to them. "What should I do?" they ask. "How should I handle this situation? What path should I take?" Yet those decisions are best decided from within, when your mind is clear and focused on your true desires.

After years of studying meditation and after many trips to India, I came to realize that I am the source of my own joy and peace. Power is not found in the hands of others but is within our own grasp. When we take our power back and begin to honor our teacher within, even more doorways open to inner knowingness. Unexplored territory is awaiting within to be excavated.

Commitment will aid the process of self mastery; the more you practice the fine art of inner listening, the more your decision-making power will increase. It is wonderful to receive wise counsel from others and use it on your journey to self mastery. Just be sure their wisdom resonates with your own. If it does, integrate it into your higher knowingness. If it doesn't, don't waste time judging or analyzing. The bottom line is honoring your own wisdom and checking your inner motivations. Is this my highest truth? Does this resonate with me? Is this wisdom in my best interest and for the greater good of all? These and the following questions will help you access your inner teacher and keep your mind well tuned to self-discovery. Celebrate and honor your teacher within; allow the classroom of life to teach you its priceless wisdom.

## Exploratory Questions for Honoring the Teacher Within

1. Do I feel guilty when I question authority?
2. Why do I silence my inner wisdom in favor of another's?
3. Can I listen to the wisdom of others and discern which part of their truth resonates with my own?
4. Am I honoring my teacher within on a daily basis? Do I focus on the master within or do I forego that voice for other masters?
5. Am I listening to and honoring my intuition?

CHAPTER 8

# Living Wide Open

*E*verywhere I go I see many people living like robots – their lives are a series of struggles, with no passion, enthusiasm or delight. Worse, this apathy and low-level depression is taken as the norm. Instead of living happily and "wide open," they function in a fog of mediocrity. Life does not have to be this way!

To live wide open, on the other hand, is to know you are the conscious creator of your own reality. Living wide open means living in the moment without conscious or unconscious preoccupation with your past or future. It implies living authentically each day and being true to yourself regardless of other's opinions. It is seeing the world with the eyes of a child, living with joy and abandon, and delighting in each new experience. To live wide open you must walk a profound path of trust, courage and self-respect.

I often tell people to "take their emergency brake off." For me, taking the emergency brake off has meant finding the wisdom and internal fortitude to stand in my truth and be who I am. Years ago, for example, I was keynote speaker for a large bankers' association. During my speech I realized I was hesitating, wondering if I should end the program with my usual unbridled, highly enthusiastic "Yes, Yes, Yes!" The exercise gets the audience to their feet shouting with me, thus taking their own emergency brakes off. It also permits the secretion of endorphins (natural mood elevators) and gets the blood and heart rate revving. I soon realized to do anything less for this speech would be a disservice to myself and to my audience. So I did the "Yes!" ending and everyone loved it, even those who maybe thought they shouldn't.

My point is that we sometimes obstruct our spontaneity and creative flow; we are too preoccupied with what we look like and with what others will think. It's getting out of our comfort zones – not staying stuck in them – that's healing and eye-opening. The bottom line is this: Don't mistake the opinions of others as your truth, or feel that others know you better than you know yourself. Shakespeare, with his consummate skill stated, "To thine own self be true." Your truths are your truths. Furthermore, your facts are your facts. A "fact" becomes a "fact" when enough information is gathered and enough people believe and agree on the data. The more people agree with the data, the more factual it becomes, yet ultimately this is an intellectual process. Remember, for centuries we thought it was a fact that the Earth was flat. Even facts change over time so be open and learn to discern your truths. We can access information from outside sources and from inside sources. In other words, listen with both your head and heart and see with your physical eyes as well as your inner eye of discernment. Honor the beliefs and truths of others, but don't be bound by them unless they resonate with your own. Don't let others dictate how you should behave. There are no two people who see or interpret the world in the same way. Even as you read this book, you will interpret these words based on your understanding, which may be different from mine. It is your interpretation, not my interpretation, that makes the difference. There are times that I may use words differently than you would; however, the important issue is that you feel the substance of the work and how it can be beneficial to you as an individual. Part of living wide open is being true to yourself in every aspect and yet allowing everyone the space to interpret the world as they see it. There are six billion people on this planet and six billion different paths; each of us has our own unique contribution to make, so make it your own.

Living wide open means observing the whole play of life and participating, actively, without reservation. You begin to realize that you are creating your own reality and setting the stage for a life filled with purpose, love and integrity. Imagine yourself as the whole play; you are the actor, the director, the writer, the stage manager, the costume designer and all the other roles that go into creating a play.

As you begin to live wide open and fathom the awesome joy and responsibility of being the whole play, your path will truly be the path of a self master. You will see the world with new eyes, not simply from an intellectual standpoint but from an inner knowing-

ness. It is your play. What kind of script do you wish to write and what picture do you want to paint that reflects the real you?

It's so invigorating to see someone who lives wide open, who is not afraid of the opinions of others and who has the courage to take the emergency brake off and let his light shine. Think of Austin Powers – Yeah, Baby!

On your journey to self-love, you must face your inner fears and demons to survive with your integrity and self-esteem intact. How? By knowing your inner landscape better than the outer landscape. By knowing the nooks and crannies of your soul, integrating the shadow and the light to create a fusion of color, sound and depth that no external influence can disturb. People who live wide open have quelled their inner fear, explored their areas of resistance and turned their perceived weaknesses into strengths. Affirm your uniqueness and live your life with joy, spontaneity, enthusiasm and laughter. Release the brakes!

## Exploratory Questions for Living Wide Open

1. Have I taken my emergency brake off or am I still holding back for fear that other people may think I am silly or stupid?
2. Do I allow myself to live wide open and be spontaneous like a child?
3. Am I delighting in my own unique approach to life or am I trying to be something I am not to please others?
4. When was the last time I did something really fun, outrageous or playful that was initially out of my comfort zone?
5. Do I "under perform" in my life by staying stuck in a fog of mediocrity?
6. Am I starring in my own play?

# THE RAY OF THE MIND

*"Where is the love, beauty and truth we seek,*
*but in our mind?"*

PERCY BYSSHE SHELLEY

CHAPTER 9

# Creating Your Own Reality

*L*ike quantum physicists probing inside the atom and investigating its structure, exploratory surgeons of the soul delve into the universal laws that underpin our existence. One such law is the law of attraction. The law of attraction simply states: *That which is likened to itself is drawn.* Like attracts like. Our thoughts are like magnets, so what we think about returns to us. Jesus said long ago, "What you sow, so shall you reap." That is the law of attraction at work; understand and employ it and your life will change.

To remedy our lives we need to investigate our thoughts. Do we spend the bulk of our time thinking about what we want or what we don't want? Be honest with yourself. Self-love asks us to celebrate our specialties and turn our vulnerabilities into strengths. We do not deny our needed areas of improvement; we simply transform them through the daily practice of self-love, exploratory soul searching and positive re-programming statements. If we continue to focus on what isn't right with ourselves or other people, we lessen the flow of our God-given creative abilities and remain stuck in fear, guilt, anger and resentment. Consciously employ the law of attraction; remember, like attracts like. Do you fear being sick? If so, be aware that by the law of attraction you may be drawing sickness to you. On the other hand, do you affirm being well? If so, smile into the knowingness that you are attracting optimal health. The law of attraction is like the law of gravity...it is ever present and always in effect. Denial, judging and blaming make us more susceptible to those negative emotions we do not want to attract. In fact, many people are adept at focusing on problems and can articulate very clearly what isn't working in the world. We desperately need people to be equally adept at solutions! Focusing on the negative cuts us off from possible solutions and makes us feel frustrated, disheartened and disil-

*"Great men are they who see that spiritual is stronger than any material force, that thoughts rule the world."*

RALPH WALDO EMERSON

lusioned. Look around you. Are people being proactive and creating viable solutions to complex problems or are they simply lamenting about what is wrong?

Self mastery requires an optimistic attitude and a strong sense of self-determination. What differentiates a self master from a self-doubter is that the self master is willing to stand in and "show up" for life and not be a passive recipient to whatever life throws his way. Self masters understand that their life is in their control. Self masters focus on solutions rather than problems. A recent international study showed that those who feel they have the most control over their lives have a 60 percent lower risk of death in any given year than those who feel helpless. Researchers found that this sense of one's own power is a major reason optimists are healthier. Conversely, studies revealed that feeling helpless is extremely stressful and can have deleterious effects on our health.

Dr. Seligman, in his book *Learned Optimism,* found that as children, pessimists developed "learned helplessness" by being encouraged to feel that they have no power over life events. This "learned helplessness" set the stage for believing the proverbial cup is half empty rather than half full. In bright contrast, optimists don't just seem better, they are better. The belief that they can improve things becomes a self-fulfilling prophecy. Optimists plan ahead and plan well because they think their ideas will work. In a related study, researchers found that people's health status depends on the way they see themselves. Self-reporting participants who saw themselves as healthy were healthy and those who saw themselves as sick were sick. (More studies are cited in Chapter 15.) The simple conclusion is that we are what we think; we often feel how we think we feel. We would be wise to employ the law of attraction to our benefit and to be optimistic about our well-being. Optimists tend to take good care of themselves because they believe in their optimal health and naturally engage in behaviors that support their beliefs. The good news is that even hard-nosed skeptics can learn to look on the bright side...without faking it. We have discussed the power of our thoughts and how to re-program a negative thought to a positive thought; that is basically the same as learned opti-

mism. By employing the law of attraction and focusing on your desired outcomes, you can increase your optimism and change from feeling helpless to being hope-filled. A common theme throughout this book is focusing on what we want rather than what we don't want. It sounds simple and obvious but it takes conscious

attention, discipline and self-love to live that truth everyday. Focus on what is right about you and others. Remember, you do not have to respond to anything by taking offense...no one or nothing can affect you unless you let them. You can learn to forgive yourself and others. End the struggle and employ the law of attraction to your advantage.

Envision that you already have what it is you desire, such as optimal health, financial/spiritual abundance, loving relationships, joy and peace. Fathom the power of mastering the law of attraction! Think about how wonderful it would be to consciously create your own reality.

## Exploratory Questions for Creating Your Own Reality

1. Are you consciously creating the life you desire?
2. Do you focus on what you want or what you don't want?
3. Are you a problem solver or a problem maker?
4. Would you define yourself as an optimist or a pessimist?
5. Do you think about how good people are or how bad people are?
6. Are you attracting joy and happiness by seeing the opportunity in all life experiences?

CHAPTER 10

# Constructing Healthy Boundaries

**W**e all must define our personal boundaries. But what are they and how do we create them? Think of boundaries as cells; they have clearly defined borders, yet are permeable. The doors of the cell (boundaries), allow it to interact with the environment as substances move across its membranes. Cells can differentiate between substances that support life and those that might be harmful. This discriminating activity is vital to their, and your, survival. Personal boundaries serve a similar function, providing a protective barrier to keep our inner sanctum and unique sense of self intact. We need personal boundaries to function as healthy individuals. It's essential to set boundaries to divert the flow of opinions and actions of others so they don't determine our state of mind.

The paradox to boundaries is we are all one; our lives are deeply intertwined and interconnected. Yet we cannot become so enmeshed in each other's lives that we lose our objectivity. Defining our personal space and standing in our power are the keys to good boundaries.

As a clinician and counselor, I learned to construct boundaries to keep from becoming overly invested and emotionally entangled in the lives of my clients. I felt almost "hard-wired" to fix and heal every soul on the planet. It took a great deal of insight to realize no one needs to be fixed or rescued. Instead, the best gift I can give anyone is the gift of themselves. To empower people with the knowledge that they are the source of their own power, that their strength comes from within, allows them to stand in their power rather than give it to another, no matter how well meaning that other person may be.

Another aspect of boundaries involves exploring where they are missing, or examining our personal boundaries to see if they need restructuring. Inquire within as to whether you are consistently setting boundaries and respectfully honoring the boundaries of others. Ask yourself, "Am I honoring my needs for peace and quiet or are they secondary to the needs of others? Do I allow my behavior to change depending on who I am with, especially my family? Do I feel as though I am being taken for granted? Do I allow other people space when they need it?"

Without healthy personal boundaries, we are like sponges soaking up the influence of others; we absorb any and all thoughts via our receptive selves. This lack of internal censoring is unhealthy and exhausting. On the other hand, be mindful not to construct inappropriate boundaries that stunt your growth and limit your experience. This may lead to walling yourself off from potentially beneficial people and situations. Honor your intuition and then act on it.

> *"Let there be spaces in your togetherness... stand together yet not too near together, for the pillars of the temple stand apart, and the oak tree and the cypress grow not in each other's shadow."*
> KAHLIL GIBRAN

Setting healthy boundaries is troublesome if you've not been socialized or enculturated to respect personal space, or to say *no*. I come from a large family with eight strong personalities. For years we lived in a Blue Bird bus with less than two feet of personal space each, to say nothing of the lack of privacy. My parents slept on the fold-down "dining room" table, separated by a thin barrier from their six children. My sister and I shared a bunk bed, as did my two younger brothers. My oldest brother and sister had their own private alcove – the size of a small closet. We all shared one bathroom with a tiny shower...imagine trying to establish clearly defined personal boundaries in this situation! Lack of physical boundaries such as these can be overcome with time and money. Defining emotional boundaries, however, is a tricky, subtle issue. It's difficult to be objective with others if you can't differentiate between their thoughts and your own. My sister Jennifer and I have always had a close relationship, raised as though we were twins and known as "the girls." Because of this constant connection, diverging on our own paths was painful and confusing. As adults we had to redefine ourselves, separating the intertwined threads of our personalities in order to appreciate our own unique sense of self.

In similar ways, we define ourselves through other people. When we are co-dependent, without healthy boundaries, we want others to be the source of our joy and contentment. If they don't behave as we expect, we feel annoyed or rejected. This type of belief makes us feel powerless rather than powerful. For most of our growing up, we were shown "power over" and "powerless" models of behavior that left us feeling unsure of which one to emulate. As a result, we got mixed messages and never formulated an understanding of what a healthy, empowered relationship looks like. In evolving co-committed relationships, power struggles cease to exist; "power over" evolves into "power with." One realizes that the source of happiness is best sought within and then shared outwardly.

## *Exploratory Questions for Creating Healthy Boundaries*

1. **Do I set clear boundaries with others and myself?**
2. **Can I say no without feeling guilty?**
3. **Do I create too many boundaries that become barriers?**
4. **Am I able to separate my thoughts from those closest to me?**
5. **Can I stand in my power even as others are not standing in their power?**

# CHAPTER 11

# Goal Setting

*T*he new millennium promises to be an era of healthy plea-
sures and a more enlightened version of success and wellness. In
these changing paradigms, it is important to keep our priorities in
perspective. Enlightened goal setting is one way to achieve our
desired intentions with focus, discipline and passion. It is the ability to pay attention without tension.

The word discipline may conjure up all kinds of
rebellious thoughts, particularly if you grew up in a
controlling environment. It's hard to maintain a discipline of exercise, for example, even though we know
such activities are good for us. Somewhere in our
early programming, we equated self-discipline with
parental discipline, and this response is consciously or
unconsciously triggered every time we begin an exercise program in earnest. It's as if we self-sabotage to
prove we will not be controlled.

> *"Many of life's
> failures are
> people who did
> not realize how
> close they were
> to success when
> they gave up."*
>
> THOMAS EDISON

These sabotaging thoughts are usually not at a
conscious level. So think about what you are thinking
about. Examine your patterns and see where the disconnection occurs. Are you setting yourself up for
failure by setting outrageous goals, such as losing 15 pounds in one
week? Are you creating undue stress by trying to make millions on
the stock market in a month? Are you trying to be all things to all
people? Relax. You won't need to beat yourself up or self-sabotage
once you "unplug" from beliefs that no longer serve you. Be gentle
with yourself. One of the best ways to re-program is to regain a
fresh perspective by affirming each day that you are a competent,
creative individual. Remember to enjoy the journey, not just the
satisfaction of reaching your goals.

## Daily Renewal

Daily renewal is a statement about how you wish your day,
and ultimately, your life, to unfold. It is your soul speaking to your
heart, your heart translating to your mind, and your mind giving

your body directions. It is ultimately an expression of self-love.

In order to gain control of your goals and fully implement them, you must first know yourself, and then know what you want. You must take responsibility for all the things in your life. The key to this step is performing it each day. This is a twenty-four-hours-a-day, seven-days-a-week job. Daily renewal begins when you awaken in the morning to thank your Creator for another beautiful day, to state what is important to you, what you wish to accomplish, and the steps you will take that day to work toward your goals. These can be long-term or immediate goals. For example, wake up in the morning and tell yourself: "I love myself unconditionally and I will do what it takes to achieve a high level of self-love." Discipline, coupled with positive affirmations, will recharge your goal setting and make it more meaningful.

## Targeted Tips for Goal Setting:

- **Believe in yourself.** Even if you have failed many times at something, believe in your ability to accomplish what you have set out to do.

- **Set a goal.** This may sound obvious, but many people set out to do something without exactly listing what it is they want to do. We make vague or unclear promises to do better, which is meant very sincerely but is not a clear goal. Goals are specific: "I will lower my cholesterol by 20 points within the next six months." "I will maintain a regular yoga exercise program three times a week." "I will make time for one fun family outing each week."

- **Make it reasonable.** If you wanted to learn to pole-vault, would you set the bar at 15 feet for your first jump? Of course not; you would never make it over the bar. It is the same with goals. Don't aim so high that you set yourself up for failure. Instead, take it easy and shoot for short-term targets you can reach.

- **Have a plan.** How are you going to reach your goals? Small, calculated steps will carry you a lot further than nebulous leaps. Instead of promising to cut all the fat from your diet, vow to switch from whole milk to soy milk. Similarly, don't tell yourself you'll exercise more; commit to walking ten minutes a day. Be specific and follow through completely on one goal before moving on to the next. Record your progress in a journal and review it often. Nothing spells success like success. Success is a fabulous motivator.

● **Focus on the benefits.** Each of us profits from the power of positive thinking and self-love, not fear, guilt or pressure. When we hear statements like "one in four women will get breast cancer," such dire statistics don't automatically motivate most women to quit smoking or change their lifestyle. Fear tactics don't work. When faced with potentially life-threatening information, it may upset us so much we reach for the nearest comfort food, such as chocolate, to medicate our anxiety. Ask yourself how you would feel if, instead of focusing on what you don't want (illness), you focused on what you do want (health). Imagine affirming that by walking ten minutes today you just prolonged your life, increased your blood flow, encouraged the release of endorphins and enjoyed some fresh air. Do you feel better framing it this way? Feel calmer, more optimistic? What you've just done is successfully re-programmed old patterning and replaced it with the power of positive thinking and positive motivation.

● **Build on past success.** We are often inspired and moved to action when we reflect on where we've been and think about all the obstacles we've overcome. Celebrate those successes and use them as fuel for continued success. Think back to something you've accomplished that made you proud, perhaps learning to play an instrument, completing some higher education or finishing a big project. This took discipline, hard work and patience but you reached your goal. If you believe it, you can achieve it!

## *Exploratory Questions for Goal Setting*

1. **Do you set clear goals and work toward completing them or do you list them but never follow through on your stated goals?**
2. **Do you persevere even if you experience setbacks?**
3. **How often do you review your goals?**
4. **Are your goals reasonable and flexible?**
5. **How do you celebrate your achievements?**

CHAPTER 12

# Living Life on Purpose

$T$he purpose of life is to live a life of purpose. Each of us has a mission. To define this purpose we need to explore our intentions. Take a moment to reflect on your purpose in life as it unfolds before you. Intentionality is our ability to act deliberately or on purpose, to say what we mean and mean what we say. Are your thoughts and actions aligned with your intentions? Often our intentions are noble but our behavior doesn't reflect them; to live your life on purpose is to bridge behavior with intentions.

*"Man's task is to become conscious of the contents that press upwards from the unconscious...as far as we can discern, the sole purpose of human existence is to kindle a light in the darkness of mere being."*

CARL JUNG

Why don't our intentions always mirror our actions? The answer is that often our spoken intentions are not our heartfelt truths or deepest desires. Are your career goals based on what you thought your parents or friends felt would be most advantageous for you? Do you make the connection between your thoughts, words, actions, internal motivations and intentions?

To answer these questions we have to increase our self-awareness and deeply explore our inner landscape. What are my intentions in life? What do I want to accomplish with my life? Am I living my life on purpose based on my mission statement or on someone else's vision? Did you want to be an artist but were told to be an engineer? Did you long to be an oceanographer but were persuaded to be an accountant?

By exploring our intentions we can consciously make decisions consistent with our personal and professional goals and core values. Our core values guide our path and keep us on track. Aligning values with intention equals freedom from stress. If you know your purpose, align with your values and act on your intentions. The result of this practice will be a life lived on purpose; the stress of wondering what your life is all about or what to do with your life will be a concern of the past.

Intentionality has several aspects, including managing distractions and remaining focused on objectives. Why do we procrastinate? Why do we tackle the easy stuff first and leave the hard stuff for later? Either we're not fully committed or we haven't transformed commitment to conviction.

*"Both life and livelihood are about living in depth, living in meaning, purpose, joy and a sense of contributing to the greater community.*
MATTHEW FOX

There is an urgency that comes with living your life on purpose, a passion to act on your heartfelt desires and make your visions a reality. Unwavering focus allows us to get what we want, and focus comes from quieting the mind and zeroing in on stated intentions to come up with an action plan. Then we need the courage to step out confidently among our peers and let our convictions lead to fruition.

Another aspect of intentionality lies in our ability to be aware of our internal motivations. Are there ulterior motives when we seek certain friendships or partnerships? Do we have unspoken expectations and unspoken motives that complicate our relationships and hinder our ability to be successful in our stated intention?

The opposite of intentionality is impulsiveness, randomly doing things haphazardly without thinking of the consequences of our actions. Don't confuse impulsiveness with spontaneity. When we act with intentionality, we accept responsibility for both our actions and our motivations.

## Steps to achieving a life lived on purpose:

● Before any major event, important meeting, family gathering or situation that warrants "pre-paving," simply pause and ask yourself, "What do I hope to achieve and what do I want to happen here?" Notice if you get any gut feelings or intuition as to what would be the best way to handle this situation and then be clear about your purpose. Act on your hunches.

● Avoid unnecessary distractions by setting aside time to complete a task, and be firm. When you need to focus on a task that requires your undivided attention, put aside anything that might interfere; keep re-directing your mind if it starts to wander. Schedule breaks and mini-retreats to focus on your breathing so your mind can be fresh. Reward yourself when you complete a big project or skillfully handle a situation.

● Question your motives and notice when you say things like "I didn't mean to say that" or "I wasn't inferring anything," or "I didn't intend for you to take it that way ;" these comments all have to do with motives and clear communication. Again, say what you mean and mean what you say. The clearer and simpler your message, the better. Be aware of the impact of your words or actions on others. People have different work ethics, beliefs and personality styles so be mindful of not inferring blame if someone works or thinks differently than you.

By living your life on purpose, you trigger the fire that ignites the force of passion within. Passion allows you to have the energy and focus to make a difference in yourself and the world. Rise from your slumber and, as my friend Bob Czimbal says, "set your life on fire and seek those who fan your flame!" Be that candle that burns brightly and know that you can and do make a difference everyday. Make it your deepest desire and highest wish to be of service, to live your life on purpose.

Go within and find the truth of your being. Allow all that is not truth to fall away with ease and grace. Having found your unique truth, live in harmony that will lead to the fulfillment of desires and expression of your divine purpose.

## Exploratory Questions for Living a Life of Purpose

1. Are your intentions aligned with your purpose?
2. Do you say what you mean and mean what you say?
3. Are you honoring your highest and best good or are you allowing your purpose in life to be defined by someone else?
4. What steps have you taken to explore your true purpose in life and how have you acted on those inner discoveries?
5. What legacy do you wish to leave through your life's work?

# THE RAY OF THE BODY

*"A healthy body is guest-chamber for the soul:
a sick body is a prison."*

FRANCIS BACON

CHAPTER 13

# Honoring the Body

**T**his chapter speaks mainly to women, because in my experience women suffer far more than men from poor body image. Many females are preoccupied with body flaws and feel deep dissatisfaction with their weight and size. Honoring your own unique body type in a culture obsessed with thinness requires self-respect. It also requires transcending the belief that we are just a body. We are far more than this physical costume and the more grounded we are in our soul consciousness, the less superficial our lives will be.

*Pierre-Auguste Renoir, Bathers*

I am not a small woman; I've never been thin nor have I always loved myself unconditionally. However, over the years I've learned to love my body for its unique talents and abilities. I now affirm everyday that I am fit, trim and beautiful. My body is muscular yet it has some fat as well. This brings to mind another myth, that people are either fit or fat. People can be both fit and fat. Physically active people are able to attain great health profiles, have increased strength and flexibility and still appear large. The opposite is true as well. Someone who appears thin but never exercises may have no stamina, a poor health profile and zero muscle tone. Size is not everything. Women tend to perpetuate the image problem more than men, comparing themselves with other women and saying things like "she shouldn't wear leggings, she's too fat for that," or "her butt's too big for that tight dress." Catch yourself when you begin to judge other women and eliminate the belief that we have to look a certain way to be attractive. If we want our daughters to see themselves as more than just a body, we must stop obsessing about ours. We are all attractive in our own right and shouldn't be judged by a scale or the fashion industry.

## Psychological Factors

Sometimes defense mechanisms are a powerful player in the weight game. Many women use weight as an insulation device, a way to keep people at bay. Some feel it's not safe to be beautiful because they fear being sexualized – seen as sexual objects rather than intelligent and multi-talented women. Striking beauty exacts its own toll; many beautiful women have told me they were considered less intelligent because of their blonde hair, good looks and sexy figure. Have you heard statements that sexualized you and found yourself putting on weight to insulate yourself? We often use defense mechanisms to keep us from feeling vulnerable or exposed. Such emotional stuffing is one of a multitude of reasons why weight problems persist. We may not be consciously aware of this behavior until someone brings it to our attention. Making the connection between sexualization and weight has helped many women let go of the illusion that a healthy weight equals unwanted attention.

Peter Paul Rubens, The Judgement of Paris

Dieting itself makes us obsessed with food, weight and appearance and often leads to lowered self-esteem. Learn to identify the emotions and situations that make you want to medicate with food and then be kind to yourself in the process. Stop doing battle with your body. Heal the part of you that feels self-conscious and simply accept who you are. Honor the differences. If you are deeply dissatisfied with your body, change it! Change your thoughts about your body as well.

Another psychological factor is how we perceive ourselves...it is hard to feel slender when you think you are fat. Remember the law of attraction; if you keep saying "I'm fat" everyday, you keep reinforcing that belief in your body and mind. The body responds to the beliefs you hold about yourself. Belief becomes biology. Rather than focusing on your weight, flab, or wrinkles, begin to celebrate your body and gently coax it into fitness. Begin to build on your strengths. If you are strong, do exercises to reinforce that skill. For example, power yoga employs all the major muscle groups and requires strength and stamina but doesn't require a high impact workout.

## Sociological Factors

No discussion of body image would be complete without a cursory glance at the impact of collective societal beliefs regarding body size and shape. There was a time in our recent past when big women were regarded as beautiful and the full-figured woman was sought after to paint or sculpt. Think of the great works of art by Rubens and Moore, who created masterpieces depicting large women. In our distant past, fertility goddesses were common and held in high esteem. Some of the earliest sculptured stone objects from more than 30,000 years ago were female figurines

*The Venus of Willendorf*

carved with emphasis on the reproductive organs, namely breasts and buttocks. These figurines are thought to represent fertility goddesses. One in particular, given the name Venus, was found in Willendorf, Austria, and replicas of her are now readily available. Another great fertility goddess from our past is Ishtar. Ishtar, or Innanna, is associated with the Mesopotamian era and is often depicted in her characteristic breast-offering pose. Cultures the world over celebrate the body feminine. Perhaps we need to rekindle our appreciation of these goddesses from ancient civilizations and re-discover our goddess within.

We have re-defined "beauty" and at present, it seems thin is in. Who is responsible for this changing perception of beauty in our culture? It appears that both men and women are responsible for the collective stereotypes we hold dear. How can we re-shape our views about beauty? One simple solution lies in changing the focus from the body to the soul. What measures do we use to detect inner beauty? Why not adopt some new standards such as "She is so beautiful because she is so compassionate and loving".... imagine being assessed by others with this as the goal. The fashion industry would be in for a shock as would the fitness industry and every other business that makes its profit off the belief that the body is the be all, end all measure of beauty.

The key is to honor your body on *all* levels. Honor your body physically, psychologically and emotionally. Little by little, you will feel completely at peace with who you are inside and out.

# Exploratory Questions for Honoring the Body

1. Do you love your body or are you constantly finding fault with it?
2. What defense mechanisms do you employ (emotional stuffing, binging, starvation, etc.) to avoid being sexualized?
3. Why do you define your sense of self by how you look or how much you weigh?
4. Do you accept your unique body type and celebrate it regardless of what society deems as beautiful?
5. What re-programming statements can you say each day that will restore compassion within so that you truly honor your body?

CHAPTER 14

# Creating Balance

**S**top, look and listen to your life. Are you juggling home, career, family and community and neglecting your spirit? Are the pieces of your puzzle out of whack?

Some workers clock in for more than 60 hours a week, while chaos runs rampant on the home front. I am currently working with a gentleman in Atlanta, a middle manager in a large multinational corporation. He averages 60 to 80 hours a week at work, sits on the board of his church, coaches his son's soccer team at school and wonders why he is exhausted at the end of the day. Are we running our lives or are our lives running us? Too often external demands are dictating our schedules. Each of us has our own approach to balance, but we all need a system that creates order in our lives. Regaining balance requires courage. We constantly have to sift through mail, e-mail, phone calls, reports, bills and other items that all clamor for our attention. We need to filter this flood of information we are inundated with daily.

> *"Fortunate, indeed, is the man who takes exactly the right measure of himself, and holds a just balance between what he can acquire and what he can use."*
>
> PETER MERE LATHAM

There is a reason for the popularity of the phrase "simplify, simplify, simplify." Put it into practice and the outcome is profound. Simplifying our lives means removing inordinate amounts of stress from our day-to-day existence. Do you really need 80 movie channels and that big house? Do you need dozens of magazine subscriptions instead of just your favorite? Why not get rid of all but one credit card to minimize debt, paper work, stress and temptation? If we are not careful, our possessions become our burdens.

When we are in balance we give the gift of a centered mind. When we are out of balance, no matter how much we want to serve, our clarity will be lacking. Balance is critical to optimal wellness. The four main areas of our overall wellness are body, mind, spirit and service. Examine these four areas of your life. Consider how much time you contribute to each. How do you feed your body? Are you eating healthy foods that support your well-being? Are you doing some form of exercise that you love and that feels good to you? Do you pamper your body with hot baths, massage or the luxury of sleeping in? Are you feeding your mind and intellect stimulating thoughts that sharpen your mental clarity? Are you keeping good company instead of surrounding yourself with negative influences that drain your energy and stifle your creativity? Is your spirit being fed by nature, silence, love, sweetness and solitude? Do you allow yourself quiet time to reflect on the mysteries of creation, the flowers, the animals, the magnificent sky and the endless ocean? Is your spirit nourished or malnourished? Do you read uplifting books and study various things to maintain your mental health? Do you value service, and what steps are you taking to share your resources with others? Do you reach out beyond your self-imposed comfort zones to serve the world through your work? Are you spending too much time serving others and neglecting yourself?

Let these questions promote a guilt-free, shameless self-inquiry. Use them to perform exploratory surgery of your soul and uncover where you are losing energy. Find your balance "leaks" in the craft of your inner self, make the necessary course corrections and judiciously guide yourself back into balance within the safe harbor of your soul.

Ultimately, we need to balance action with reflection, head with heart, work with play, masculine with feminine, truth with compassion and love with wisdom. We need to listen again to that quiet voice within. We must reunite all the myriad parts of ourselves into wholeness. We need to realign and reunite our masculine and feminine energies within and shine the light of love on our shadow side. We need to continually remind ourselves to stop seeking outside ourselves for validation of self-love, self worth or a sense of belonging. Each of us has within us all the required tools, skills, and wisdom to be happy, abundant, healthy, balanced, suc-

*"What I dream of is an art of balance, of purity and serenity devoid of troubling or depressing subject matter – a soothing, calming influence on the mind, something like a good armchair which provides relaxation from physical fatigue."*

HENRI MATISSE

cessful and fully conscious spiritual beings. Enlightenment is not out there somewhere; it is within you. We simply need to re-discover our inner beauty, our inner wisdom and stop separating ourselves.

Examine all the areas of your life that are out of balance. Where there is disharmony and disunity, allow the light of your Higher Self to gently guide you to those areas that need attention. By integrating our inner selves and embracing all parts of ourselves we can then restore balance to the whole self. Achieving balance creates a state of wholeness, unshakeability and equanimity.

## Exploratory Questions for Creating Balance

1. Do I balance work and play?
2. Am I spending enough quality time with my family?
3. What do I do to keep myself in balance (massages, hot baths, family night out, etc.)?
4. Am I spending quality time with myself without feeling guilty?
5. Have I integrated my masculine and feminine sides and balanced my shadow side with my light side so that I feel whole inside and out?

CHAPTER 15

# Belief Becomes Biology

*T*hroughout the course of history we have toyed with the idea of psychosomatic healing or psychosomatic illness. It is referenced in countless literary classics and antiquated medical tomes. Through the ages, a dominant thought prevailed, "As a man thinketh, so he is." The heart of many spiritual teachings, both Eastern and Western, is the belief in the power of our thoughts to create physical health or disease, depending on belief. I will share with you a story from Yogananda's book, *Autobiography of a Yogi*, in which he recounts a story about his teacher Sri Yukteswar. When he was younger, Yukteswar had become seriously ill and lost a considerable amount of weight. While rehabilitating, he visited his guru, Lahirei Mahasaya, and shared with him why he was sick. On hearing his story, Mahasaya said, "So, you made yourself sick and now you think you are thin. But I am sure you will feel better tomorrow." The next day Yukteswar did feel much better and thanked him. Mahasaya said, "Your condition was quite serious, and you are still frail, who knows how you will feel tomorrow." Like prophecy, the next day Yukteswar did indeed feel frail and weak and Mahasaya said, "So, you once again indispose yourself." Slowly Yukteswar began to see a pattern develop. He noticed

> *"Macbeth: 'Canst thou not minister to a mind diseased, pluck from the memory a rooted sorrow, raze out the written troubles of the brain, and with some sweet oblivious antidote cleanse the stuffed bosom of that perilous stuff which weighs heavy upon the heart?' Doctor: 'Therein the patient must minister to himself.'"*
>
> WILLIAM SHAKESPEARE

that his ups and downs corresponded to Mahasaya's statements and realized his guru was trying to teach him a very valuable lesson. Mahasaya said, "One day you say to me, 'I am well,' and the next day you say, 'I am sick.' It isn't that I have been healing or indisposing you. It is your own thoughts that have made you alternately weak and strong." Yukteswar asked, "If I think I am well and that I have regained my former weight, will it be so?" Mahasaya responded, "It is so." Within moments Yukteswar felt his strength return and within a few days he regained almost 40 pounds! Belief becomes biology.

Paradigms are changing rapidly in the field of health and wellness. A new science of body/mind is emerging. Research scientists and physicians have traditionally seen the immune system as separate from the workings of the mind and the behaviors of the body. From the time of Descartes to the present we have been trained to see the body as a complex, biological machine, fine honed by millions of years of evolution, completely separate from the mind.

Psychoneuroimmunology is a relatively new term coined by Dr. Robert Ader in the early 1980's. Ader and other researchers of late have discovered a powerful link between body and mind. Psychoneuroimmunologists investigate the complex relationships between psychological and emotional factors, the brain, hormones, immunity and disease. This chapter by no means attempts a definitive explanation of the field of psychoneuroimmunology. Research turns up new discoveries each month and the field is expanding daily. My main focus has been on how our thoughts affect our immune system and how our beliefs become biology. Our minds and bodies are affected by light and dark, temperature, time of day, food; yet they are also affected by cultural beliefs, prayers, emotions and our own inner perceptions. One pioneer who has delved deeply into this emerging field is the late Norman Cousins. After surmounting incredible odds and writing about the benefits of laughter in his best-selling book, *Anatomy of an Illness*, Norman went on to write, *Head First; The Biology of Hope and the Healing Power of the Human Spirit*. He explored the limited body of research, seeking to reaffirm and amplify the role that positive emotions play in enhancing the immune system, and he encouraged researchers to further investigate the benefits of positive emotions.

Medical literature is replete with studies of the negative effects of stress on the body or how anger affects us, but comparably little evidence exists to show how positive emotions such as love, hope and faith affect the body. Before we explore further into how belief becomes biology, first let us examine the components of the immune system. The main players in immunity are the brain, spleen, thymus gland, bone marrow and lymph nodes. We know now through research that the immune system is not confined or localized to one area of the body; the system is inextricably linked to all parts of our body and communication appears to be non-stop.

Imagine waking up each morning with a clear vision of your optimal health and well-being. Visualize before you go to sleep at night that while you sleep, your entire immune system is being fine-tuned for optimal performance. If you wake up in the morning and think you are sick and tired, how are you going to feel? Sick and tired. If you wake up in the morning and think that you are the embodiment of wellness, how are you going to feel? Well! Belief becomes biology. Bio - chemist Candice Pert calls this dialogue and information sharing "the molecules of emotion," saying that "Why we feel the way we feel is the result of the symphony and harmony of our own molecules of emotion that affect every aspect of our physiology, producing blissful good health or miserable disease."

*"The immune system is a mirror to life, responding to its joy and anguish, its exuberance and boredom, its laughter and tears, its excitement and depression, its problems and prospects. Scarcely anything that enters the mind doesn't find its way into the workings of the body. Indeed, the connection between what we think and how we feel is perhaps the most dramatic documentation of the fact that mind and body are not separate entities but part of a fully integrated system."*
NORMAN COUSINS

Every thought manifests. For example, if you experience negative emotional states such as anger, fear, or sadness, then these states of mind cause immune suppression. Negative, stressful thoughts affect the production of T-cells which are important immune cells found in the thymus gland. An interesting study done by researchers Kiecolt-Glaser and Glaser revealed how the stress of taking exams on medical students resulted in immune suppression as detected by blood samples taken before and after

*"Illness and disease are the opposites of health and wellness, and are made manifest in your reality at your behest. You can not be ill without at some level causing your-self to be, and you can be well again in a moment by simply deciding to be."*

CONVERSATIONS WITH GOD,
AN UNCOMMON DIALOGUE, BOOK I,
NEALE DONALD WALSCH

(Psychosomatic Medicine, Vol. 46, No. 1, Jan/Feb 1984). Conversely, if you experience positive emotions such as hope, joy, happiness and peace your immune system will benefit from increased T-cell production.

Another fascinating area of research is the investigation of the placebo effect. Medical researchers are showing how the mind converts ideas and expectations into biochemical realities. For example, Dr. Ader and colleagues found that when patients with high blood pressure were taken off drugs and treated with placebos, they maintained normal blood pressures longer than patients who were taken off active medication and treated with nothing. It seems the natural conclusion from placebo research and related mind/body studies that belief becomes biology. This does not negate the need for medical care nor does it infer that we purposely make ourselves sick. It is far more subtle and complex, but we do know that the mind has an integral role in the well-being of the body and the body has an integral role in the well-being of the mind. For me, the most important conclusion to this research is that we have a very powerful tool at our fingertips...our own mind.

We should employ our mind in the service of our overall health and wellness by focusing on our health, not illness. Having said that, if illness does arise, one is not to feel as though one has done something wrong or is paying penance; simply allow the body to heal. We have a tendency to suppress our immune system even further from *over-medicating and under-meditating.* It would be wise for us to simply allow ourselves to be in a space of healing. Even if your body aches, remember, eventually, this too shall pass. By getting stressed out about our illness or focusing on what we don't want, we take our attention off our recovery. You do not need to be the wall against the wind nor the dam in the river, simply allow the temporary discomfort to flow by. By allowing yourself to simply be in the illness you can discover the roots of it and ascertain why you might be ill. Have you been working too hard, do you need a break? Are you out of balance? We discover how to elicit our own inner pharmacy when we allow ourselves to go within and gently observe the inner workings of our minds.

Our minds are magnificent tools of creation and we are capable of immense wonder and well-being or grave illness and poor health. We need to consciously use our divine minds and believe in our ability to be well. We must be willing to be well and live fully each day. We need to train our minds to boost and maintain our natural immune system via meditation and positive re-programming statements. We need to restore the complete connection between the right and left hemispheres of our brain to its natural whole brain state, so it becomes far more receptive to new information and heightened awareness. You are creating and maintaining a healthy body. Therefore, don't give your energy to disease; instead, visualize and feel that you are well, whole and perfect. See your immune system functioning at an optimal level and affirm your wellness daily, thereby transforming your belief into your biology.

## *Exploratory Questions for Belief Becomes Biology*

1. **Am I focusing on my wellness or illness?**
2. **Do I support my body and mind by believing that health is my birthright and wellness is only a thought away?**
3. **Have I celebrated my well-being or have I lamented about what is not right with my body?**
4. **Am I allowing my immune system to operate naturally or do I suppress it with drugs that are a quick fix?**
5. **What am I doing to boost my immunity and increase my overall feeling of well-being?**

# THE RAY OF SERVICE

*"The purpose of life is undoubtedly to know oneself. We cannot do it unless we learn to identify ourselves with all that lives. The sum total of that life is God. The instrument of this knowledge is boundless, selfless service."*

MAHATMA GANDHI

CHAPTER 16

# Restoring Unity

*U*nited we stand, divided we fall. How did such a profound truth get disregarded in the "me" generation, and, for that matter, the course of human history? When did we buy into the collective belief system that "bigger is better," "only the strong survive," "might is right," "we're better, stronger, faster,"... and so on?

> *"Love alone is capable of uniting living beings in such a way as to complete and fulfill them, for it alone takes them and joins them by what is deepest in themselves."*
> PIERRE TEILHARD DE CHARDIN

If humanity is to usher in a new era of enlightenment, the foundation of that era needs to be unity, oneness and a deep desire for the collective well-being of our entire planet. We no longer can operate in isolation or superiority thinking, but must come together as one family with a divine cause to end the suffering of so many and collectively heal this beloved planet.

Such "unity thinking" involves setting aside our judgments, separations, threats (real or perceived), fears, hatred, insecurities and "what's in it for me" mentality and truly come to the table of life as a committed participant. As each of us does this, we create a positive "collective consciousness" that will uplift the world and ourselves. We adopt a new language, the *language of unity*, rather than the language of separation.

We cannot underestimate the power of collective consciousness and joint "will" to transform the world. We used to believe the world was flat; we now see it as round. We used to believe the sun revolved around the earth; we know now the earth revolves around the sun. We used to believe that war was the only way to resolve conflict; we know now we can resolve conflict through peace. We used to have walls that separated countries; now we have monuments to the past and avenues to the future. We used to live in fear and limitation; now we are experimenting with love, abundance and no limit living. Let us boldly continue this experiment. Imagine what the next century could bring if we came together in unity to create peace and harmony.

Let us let go of our old illusions. Letting go allows us to see the extent of confusion that surrounds us. By learning and observing we can then clear the fog from our eyes and see the world anew. We can discover our own truth and learn to speak from our hearts; we can live our truths and completely change our lives. Every step to increased clarity allows us to alter our collective consciousness and expand it outwardly in a positive direction.

We are making a difference. People, countries and nations are shifting to a more spiritual perspective. With increased awareness comes increased dissatisfaction with the world as it is. We are becoming more conscious of our environment. We are becoming aware of suffering on all levels. We are witnessing the disparity of the "haves" and the "have nots." We observe world hunger while tons of food are disposed of daily in wealthy nations. We notice that millions have little or no access to health care or life-saving medicines. Our hearts still ache when we see pain and suffering raging on a global scale. We wonder why some die at a young age or tragedy seems to strike sweet and innocent ones. We must be mindful to temper this newfound clarity with a passion for transforming the world as it is, lest the suffering overwhelm us. We must not turn away from the plight of the world but be compassionate and do everything we can to lessen the suffering of others. None of this suffering is the will of God and no one is being punished. We are reminded of the gift of free will and inspired to make a difference. We are reminded that our lives are an outpicturing of our thoughts so we let our thoughts lift and bless. We remember the power of adversity and what incredible things can happen when people polarize around a cause, be it to end world hunger or world war. Every experience, no matter how tragic, can be used to deepen our awareness, to uplift and inspire others.

Recall how we all witnessed the ushering in of this new millennium without any war or bloodshed or even computer problems. Millions around the globe were united in global meditations, prayers and joyful celebrations. Armed with this knowledge of the power of unity, we can remove the barriers and genuinely love our brothers and sisters the world over.

A sign of our growing unity consciousness will be that we will see each other with new eyes. We will recognize the greatness that lies in each of us. We will appreciate the smallest among us as well as the most acclaimed because each has a unique contribution to make; each is an intricate part of the cosmic puzzle. The reality is that each of us comes from diverse backgrounds and different origins, yet none is more or less important. We are all One; we are all part of the Divine. We must desist from duality thinking and release the hold duality has over us. It requires birthing a new awareness, a new unity. We as a global family need to respect all life, reject violence and learn to truly share with one another. We need to unite!

*"Just as the wave cannot exist for itself, but must always participate in the swell of the ocean, so we can never experience life by ourselves, but must always share the experience of life that takes place all around us."*
ALBERT SCHWEITZER

We are beginning to awaken from our slumber and address and ameliorate these problems. We are beginning to believe in ourselves again. We are beginning to know that we *can* make the world a better place.

When we see unity in all things, we will then be able to understand the unity of the universe. Those who see unity in all things feel the need to communicate that understanding. Self masters understand the power of collective consciousness and jointly work toward restoring unity.

Remember to utilize the power of positive, collective action and see that fragmentation and separation around the world are rapidly becoming a disease of the past because we have discovered the vaccine of unity, thereby restoring health to the world.

## Exploratory Questions for Restoring Unity

1. How am I creating harmony in my life?
2. Do I work toward re-uniting all parts of myself, or am I still battling within?
3. Am I tolerant of other people who are different than I?
4. Do I promote peace or do I encourage discord?
5. What steps am I taking to restore unity in my family, my community, and the world?

73

# ONE

One song can spark a memory
One flower can waken dreams
One tree can start a forest
One bird can herald the spring
One smile can start a friendship
One handicap can lift a soul
One star can guide a ship at sea
One speech can set a goal
One vote can change a nation
One sunbeam can light a room
One candle can erase the darkness
One laugh can chase the gloom
One step must start each journey
One word must start each prayer
One hope can raise the spirits
One prayer can show you care
One can make a difference
And that one is you
Individually and collectively
You can. You do.

ANONYMOUS

# CHAPTER 17

# Dissolving Concepts, Restoring Compassion

*I*t is virtually impossible for clear communication to occur when we are so tied to a concept that we defend the concept over individuals! Between two opposing parties, be they individuals, communities or nations, there can be no clear communication when we are ready to kill each other over a concept. Many wars, fights and personal assaults have occurred, not so much because the individuals were hostile toward one another, but because the concept, which they chose as their core belief, conflicted with the concepts of another.

> *"The only justification we have to look down on someone is if we are about to pick him up."*
>
> JESSE JACKSON

Clear communication cannot exist within concepts of competition and separation. Clear, compassionate communication cannot be experienced when based upon feelings of inferiority, superiority, alienation, separation, inadequacy, fears or other limiting beliefs. Honest communication cannot occur if you feel your security, lifestyle or freedom of expression are being threatened. Clear communication must first set the stage whereby threats are removed. This action allows for the flow of words rather than the flow of emotions. We need to set aside concepts for the sake of communication, for the sake of coming together.

For example, I may believe in principle that eating meat causes suffering to animals, but if I fought or killed people who chose to eat meat, I am defending a concept over an individual. The very essence of compassionate, masterful communication lies in the ability to suspend judgment, to remove separation consciousness, threats and pre-conceived biases and to listen with an open mind. When you communicate with others, speak not for the sake of putting your beliefs upon another or defending yourself against another's beliefs, but for the sake of honest communication. The desired result will be increased understanding followed by peace and harmony. For when one understands the other's perspective,

joint perspectives can be acknowledged and collective decisions can be brought forth.

Rather than framing it as "me and my concepts and ideas" versus all others, I can choose to widen my scope and listen to the concepts and ideas of others. I am not saying you need to abandon your stance on an issue; I am merely advocating you be willing to communicate with an open mind. In this way, we can then share our lives and feelings with others...even if we have very divergent viewpoints.

We have all heard the phrase, "walk a mile in my shoes, then and only then can you fully understand." There is great depth behind this point. It is difficult to take a stand in opposition with another when you fully understand his position. We need to listen to understand rather than just desiring to be understood.

Let us restore compassion by becoming empathetic to the plight of our global family. By integrating our inner selves and embracing all parts of ourselves we can then embrace all parts of our global family. We have a responsibility to preserve this planet and be good stewards of the land and good caretakers of one another. By coming together with these shared values, our future will be an opportunity to rediscover solidarity and deepen our understanding of unity. Perhaps these courageous acts will rewrite the wrongs of the past and change the course of history. The future is the past rewritten.

*"Full of love for all things in the world, practicing virtue in order to benefit others, this man alone is happy."*

BUDDHA

I firmly believe compassionate communication is a viable key that will unlock the doorway to peace and harmony. History has shown us that the use of power, authority, aggression and control have fostered greed, hatred, lust and corruption which in turn has created chaos, violence, disharmony and dis-unity. By employing the concepts that seek to build unity and understanding, we will dissolve

> "Kindness in
> words creates
> confidence.
> Kindness in
> thinking creates
> profoundness.
> Kindness in
> giving creates
> love."
> LAO TSU

the barriers to peace and co-create justice for all. By
deepening our self-love, we rekindle the passion for selfless service
and restore compassion with our self and the world.

## Exploratory Questions for Dissolving Concepts and Restoring Compassion

1. Do I put my concepts before people?
2. Am I willing to allow others to believe differently than I do?
3. Do I communicate with compassion and seek to understand rather than simply to be understood?
4. Am I willing to practice random acts of kindness and make the world a better place?

77

# Enlightened Leadership

## THE BUILDERS

### HENRY WADSWORTH LONGFELLOW

All are architects of Fate,
Working in these walls of Time;
Some with massive deeds and great,
Some with ornaments of rhyme.
Nothing useless is, or low;
Each thing in its place is best;
And what seems but idle show
Strengthens and supports the rest.
For the structure that we arise,
Time is with materials filled;
Our todays and yesterdays
Are the blocks with which we build.
Truly shape and fashion these;
Leave no yawning gaps between;
Think not, because no man sees,
Such things will remain unseen.
In the elder days of Art,
Builders wrought with greatest care
Each minute and unseen part;

For the gods see everywhere.
Let us do our work as well,
Both the unseen and the seen;
Make the house where gods
    may dwell
Beautiful, entire, and clean.
Else our lives are incomplete.
Standing in these walls of Time,
Broken stairways, where the feet
Stumble, as they seek to climb.
Build today, then, strong and sure,
With a firm and ample base;
And ascending and secure
Shall tomorrow find its place.
Thus alone can we attain
To those turrets, where the eye
Sees the world as one vast plain,
And one boundless reach of sky.

*A*s we enter the 21st century, leaders will begin to emerge who will lead from the heart. Leading from the heart requires the ability to listen deeply to the needs of others. Enlightened leaders employ the faculties of the mind in a balanced way, with compassion and humility. We are entering an era of enlightened leadership, in which the leader will also be the trustee who leads by example, with integrity and vision. Joel Barker, author of *Future Edge*, defines a leader as "someone who will take you to a place you would not normally go." Enlightened leadership requires courage and a passion for the pure potentiality of the future.

Enlightened leaders practice their art on the canvas of their own lives. Like a rare oil painting, enlightened leaders add color and texture on the backdrop of an often drab and colorless modern landscape. They are adept at handling multiple agendas and complex personalities. They see service as a vital ingredient to excellent leadership and know that one cannot lead without service as a core value.

*"One must be a servant of servants, and must accommodate a thousand minds. There must not be a shade of jealousy or selfishness, then you are a leader."*
SWAMI VIVEKANANDA

This level of enlightened leadership requires discipline to continually work toward self mastery. We all know about the value of non-violence, but it took the example and commitment of Mahatma Gandhi to convert this value into a reality thereby freeing India from British rule. We all know the value of compassion, but it took the example of Mother Teresa to deepen our understanding of the power of compassion and selfless service displayed day in and day out in the leper colonies of Calcutta. We all know the value of equality, we know that each person should be valued regardless of economic status or ethnicity, but it took the powerful example and vision of Martin Luther King, Jr. to articulate the dream of racial equality.

What do these great leaders share in common? They each held a profound, personal commitment to their vision of a better world. They spoke and acted from their heart and transcended the theory of social action or civil rights into a living, breathing, heartfelt mission. It was their life's work. They translated their inner truths to outer manifestations that literally changed the course of human history.

You, too, are a change agent, an architect of change building bridges to the future. Each has the potential to be an enlightened leader. Simply lead by example, teach through role modeling and sculpt the future with hands guided by an inner wisdom.

Peter Senge, author of *The Fifth Discipline: The Art and Practice of a Learning Organization*, writes that the role of a leader is this: "Leaders are designers, teachers and stewards. These roles require new skills: the ability to build shared vision, to bring to the surface and challenge prevailing mental models, and to foster more sys-

79

> *"If we do not lay out ourselves in the service of mankind who should we serve?"*
>
> ABAGAIL ADAMS

temic patterns of thinking. In short, leaders in learning organizations are responsible for building organizations where people are continually expanding their capabilities to shape the future – that is, leaders are responsible for learning." And learn we must if we are to adapt to the ever-changing world around us. Ignorance keeps us trapped in the darkness of limited thinking while knowledge frees us to shine the light on limitless possibilities.

The natural progression for an individual on the path to self mastery is to become an enlightened leader. The journey to self-love extends beyond the self to include the entire universe. In the book of our lives, service should be woven into every chapter and threaded through every paragraph.

Lead with your heart and allow each day to guide you to a place of service. Giving of yourself is a great gift indeed, but sharing the gift of self-love and empowering others to do the same is priceless.

## *Exploratory Questions for Enlightened Leadership*

1. Am I leading only with my head or am I leading with my heart as well?
2. Do I set a good example each day for consistently making choices that reflect my inner strength of character?
3. What steps am I taking to bring my leadership style to a new level?
4. Am I building shared vision with my co-workers, family and friends or do I desire all the power and glory?
5. How do I demonstrate my leadership skills and who are my mentors that inspire me to lead with an enlightened consciousness?

## Section II

# Stories That Light the Way

*"The journey of a thousand miles starts with the first step."*

LAO TSU

CHAPTER 19

# Stories that Heal

*H*aving an inner awakening is much like having a baby; the process takes time to gestate, needs nourishment and patience, and there are even labor pains in the growth spurts...but the outcome is miraculous.

The women featured in this section are seemingly ordinary women who have achieved extraordinary self-transformation by choosing to open themselves up to a new way of thinking, perceiving, living and loving. These women are from diverse backgrounds, different ethnicities, different education levels, professions and ways of thinking. Yet they all share one thing in common: A deep desire to change.

I've had the pleasure of working closely with each of these women through weekly "meditation for stress reduction" classes, women's wellness retreats and our wellness center. They have explored their inner landscape with a laser light of truth and love and surgically removed beliefs that kept them from their brilliance.

Why would anyone want to do exploratory surgery of the soul? Why would anyone "elect" to have any surgery? Because there is some source of pain or discomfort and the surgeon wants to discover the source of the distress. Exploratory surgery of the soul is about uncovering our hidden resentment, cutting away carcinogenic thoughts and shining the laser of love on our inner congestion. We need to explore the sources of our stress and allow the blood of life, love, to flow freely through our veins.

Some of the most important aspects of opening to a new reality are a hunger for truth, a passion for growth and a deep desire to change. Sometimes our greatest growth spurts happen during times of crisis, loss or tragedy. Instead of focusing on the obstacles, choose to focus on the opportunities life holds for us. We can turn all problems into teachers simply by changing our perceptions. In our weekly meditation class I often remind my class and myself that stress is a crisis of perception. Two people may experience the same event but experience it totally differently based on their perception or perspective. Change your perception and you change your reality. Change your thoughts and you change your life.

One of the biggest catalysts for my own self-transformation happened when I was 18 years old. My father died of a massive heart attack while on vacation. The event was catastrophic; my family and I were all caught off-guard by the suddenness of his passing at the young age of 49. My mother and my five other siblings were devastated. It seemed as though the sun had gone out of the solar system. This event stirred within me a deep desire to explore death and dying, reincarnation, God, the meaning of life and my own mortality. I had just finished my first year of college and did not feel I had a good understanding of death and dying so I decided to work for Hospice. I read the works of Elizabeth Kubler Ross and related experts to explore the mystery in more detail. What I discovered during that time was that we need to embrace death as we embrace life, as two sides of the same coin. I then began to ponder my own mortality and realized that if I did not change some of my Type A behaviors (striving, over-achieving, controlling) then I too could suffer the same fate as my father. My brother Paul, who was completing his M.D/PhD. program at Harvard University, was kind enough to send me a copy of Dr. Herbert Benson's book, *The Relaxation Response*, which proved quite useful. I also had the good fortune of learning about meditation in one of my courses at the University of South Florida and my life has never been the same since. Learning to meditate, slow down and breathe was no small feat for a Type A such as myself. I wanted to be perfect overnight, master meditation and be totally free of any negativity in no time! Luckily, someone along the way reminded me that self-transformation is a process; a process that takes a lifetime, with the journey being what it is all about. And so it is with this section, a journey of powerful women who defied the odds, who let their lights shine and took their power back. Let them inspire you to be the powerful creator you are. Feel, empathize, and enjoy their stories as they share them in their own voice. There is no greater teacher than experience. Let their stories light your way.

The Genius of Navigation

CHAPTER 20

# MARY'S JOURNEY
## From Tragedy to Transformation

**O**n a glorious day in late July, 1984, my husband and I were sitting with our young son in his apartment when our avid basketball player suggested a "pick-up game." My husband, always up for a contest of any kind, agreed. They changed into their shorts, T-shirts and sneakers and headed off for the gym. As they walked toward the door, my husband said with a wicked grin, "c'mon son, let's show those young upstarts how this game is played." Those were the last words I ever heard him speak. Joe died of a massive heart attack that afternoon while playing basketball. He was 49 years old, and the father of six children between the ages of 17 and 25.

In the space of a few hours our lives changed forever. Tragedy can sometimes motivate a positive change. Freud believed that of all of the defenses, sublimation, "when you turn something bad into something positive," is the most mature and healthy of our defense mechanisms. And we do need our defense mechanisms to deal with loss whether it is a lost love, a divorce, or the ultimate loss, death.

We all have choices – we can remain stuck in loss, wallow in our self-pity or "why me's?" or we can move on. It is in moving on/changing gears that we gain strength, motivation and purpose once again.

Some people turn to their jobs, some to their network of family and friends, and some turn to drugs and alcohol to deaden the pain. When my young husband died, my salvation was my family and their enthusiastic support in my subsequent decision to return to college after a thirty-year absence. With the help of my children, I quit my job as a cashier and filled out all the necessary forms, applied to an all-women's college in the Northeast, requested financial aid and awaited the outcome. We were all so excited when the affirmative acceptance letter arrived! But when I first began my studies in earnest, the euphoria abated. I was frightened and angry. I felt sorry for myself...why me? Why my husband and not some mean person?

I was sad and worried too for my children who had lost their father in the prime of his life, in the beginning of their anxious yet exhilarating move into adulthood. Who would help me help them emotionally, financially and physically? I felt as if a giant tractor had plowed over my chest, that if I pulled up my shirt the huge treads would be there as evidence. But often there is no outward evidence of pain.

The anxiety and angst one feels, the frustration and sorrow cannot be measured in a vial or on a chart. So despite my fear and misgivings, I did what women have done for centuries...I went to work. I threw myself into my studies and learned to like my new surroundings, a tiny apartment in a small quaint college town. I was living alone for the first time in my 48 years. Having grown up in a family of eleven children and raising six of my own, one might have thought this situation heavenly. But I was wary of each new experience, each new assignment, each new friendship and I missed my family acutely. It was one of my new friends, herself a mother with grown children, who introduced me to the maxim "fake it till you make it." Here we were, women old enough to be our fellow classmates' mothers (even grandmothers) vying for grades with the "cream of the crop" of young women scholars. But because of our age, these sweet young things assumed we were far more knowledgeable, that we had more "book learning," when in fact what we had was "life experiences." We used this miracle to work even harder, to live up to those high expectations, to "make it."

This motto led me to an inner strength, a self-confidence I didn't know I owned. With a full scholarship and a part-time job in one of the campus libraries (and financial help from my children and siblings – my mom, then 88 years old, bought my text books for me each semester) I graduated from college! Along with the hard-won formal diploma from a prestigious Ivy League college came many new life skills. I realized that I had made choices every day. I had gained confidence in myself as an individual. The tragedy of my husband's death had forced me to change my life path, had forced me to the realization that I had the strength, I had the wisdom, I had the compassion, but most of all, I had love – for and from my

# Realization
# External forces
# Appreciation
# People

family, friends, classmates and mentors – love that leaves you with riches you can draw on for the rest of your life.

In my transformation, in the awakening of my soul, I was guided by several principles. I call it the REAP process:

1. Realization
2. External forces
3. Appreciation
4. People

## Briefly this means:

1. Realization of the need to change, adjust, adapt, get on with your life.

2. External forces are the forces such as economic situation, age, health, physical location, etc. These are often not circumstances we can change, so we learn to work with what we do have.

3. Appreciation is acknowledgement of self, understanding that you can, in fact, make changes; you can survive on your own.

4. People, the key support, the backbone, both those who help and guide you and those you help or assist, for in reaching out to others we help ourselves.

Ordinary life is rife with miracles if only we look for them. There's the obvious...newborns, green growing things, the love of a good person or persons. I see it in the dawn as the sun creeps skyward as I drive to work each morning, (yes, I still go to work every day). I see it in my grandchildren as they grow and thrive, struggle and excel before my very eyes. I see it in my adult children as they laugh with one another...or sometimes cry...when reminiscing about their early life, their father's eccentricities or his sense of humor. I see it as the evening closes in when I might discern my Mom's sweet face in a cloud formation.

I am not unaware that life is also rife with dangers but we need to concentrate on the good, look for the "miracles." By making a choice to focus on the positive, we can transform our lives. And indeed, it takes courage to change; many of us, like myself, are creatures of habit. It is often frightening to move out of our familiar environs with its comfortable perimeters, its easy familiarity. But change we must, particularly when dealing with a grave loss such as death. We must find a reason to go on living, a motivation to get up each morning. We must learn new skills; learn new ways of doing and being. We must take on things that we may fear and in doing so we often find that these frightening paths are not that at all.... merely different.

I am now 62 years young, still working at a job I love at a state university library. I have experienced much in my life thus far – acute pain, much happiness and many triumphs. The sustaining force for me has been family, most particularly my six children. In your children, as in a fine painting, your efforts remain long after you've gone. And from your children you can gain strength from their confidence in you. They see you initially as their whole universe, as *Mom*, teacher, soother of hurts, bestower of justice. But later, as they age, they begin to see you as a separate entity, as someone's daughter, sister, wife and friend. And at this stage of our lives, and theirs, it is appropriate and healthy to branch out, to make choices, to move beyond pain and embrace a new way of life on whatever path appeals to us. As some clever woman once knowingly said, "Be happy, it's a way of being wise."

CHAPTER 21

# GLORIA'S JOURNEY
# From Powerless to Powerful

*I* was 6 when my parents died from tuberculosis. It was hard being black and poor in the south in the 1930's, but having no mother and father was much worse. From as early as I can remember, I felt alone and abandoned.

After the death of my parents, I went to stay with my aunt who lived in Birmingham, Alabama. My aunt was a firm, strict woman. I had three older brothers and they practically raised themselves. Life was hard for me as a young girl. Early every morning I'd milk the cows and tend to the farm animals – and worry about being raped. Since I was 11 I'd been raped over and over. But no one believed me until I turned up pregnant. The father of my first child was my cousin's husband.

I had my first child at the age of 15, just a child myself; I knew I couldn't raise this child alone. Luckily my aunt helped to raise my daughter.

The raping didn't stop. I was pregnant a year later and had my first son when I was 17. I was sexually abused almost daily from the age of 11 to 17. I felt joyless, used, abused and worthless. I ended up going to Knoxville, Tennessee with a house painter when I was about 20. I'd thought he'd offer me a better life, but come to find out, he was already married. He told me he wasn't married and then his wife came and caught us in bed and that was it.

It's funny where we end up and meet people. I thought I had found the love of my life in Knoxville and we were married in 1960. It was a happy time.

I had two more children, a girl and a boy, and two who died at birth. Years into the marriage, my husband began to abuse me. He burned me, beat me, and made me feel powerless. Once I became so angry I shot him in the leg and had to do jail time. After almost 20 years of marriage, we divorced.

I later re-married. As with many marriages, the beginning years were good; we'd talk, share hobbies, support one another, and enjoy each other's company, but through the years, he too became physically and emotionally abusive. I knew deep down inside that something had to change or I was going to die.

I turned to food for comfort...junk food, high fat food, stuff that was cheap and available. I gained 150 pounds, and I could feel each pound on my knees, back and whole body. At my heaviest weight (350 pounds) and lowest point, I knew something had to give.

*Author's note: I'll never forget the day Gloria called me. I was the director of a health education center and we had just published an article in the paper about getting fit for the new year. We were encouraging people to attend a low-impact aerobics class. When Gloria called, she asked if it was okay for a black woman to attend the class. My heart almost broke! I immediately said, of course, we would love to have her come! Gloria reluctantly came walking in with a cane and a look of despair. She then began the long journey of healing herself. Over the course of 18 months, she lost almost 100 pounds, increased her self-esteem, ditched the cane, learned meditation and even got off her high blood pressure medication. At one of my women's wellness retreats, she realized just how powerless she had become and began to tap into her pain and loneliness and began to heal her wounds.*

*She had to realize the pain of betrayal, loss, rape, and sorrow that she carried within her heart and let it out. By sharing her pain, she opened herself to the support of others and ended her feelings of isolation and separation.*

*As she proudly pronounced, "I Took my power back!"*

## Gloria's tools for transformation are:

1. The importance of daily prayer and faith in God

2. My family

3. Being involved in the community, especially my women's group at the church and singing in the choir

4. Regular exercise, walking

5. Positive thinking

Chapter 22

# KAITLIN'S JOURNEY
# From Fear to Faith

$A$s a health care professional, you tend to push yourself, to go beyond your normal limits to care for others...sometimes you pay the cost with your own body. Not only did I become ill, I discovered the other side of medicine and deepened my appreciation for the trauma that patients endure while trying to become well.

In 1991, I graduated from mid-wifery school with a master's degree in nursing and set off with my husband and three small children to California to practice my craft. I was stationed at an Air Force base and immediately became involved in the primary care of pregnant women. Since my unemployed husband was taking care of the home front, it was not uncommon for me to work 80 to 100 hours a week.

I was traveling to a nursing conference in San Diego with a fellow nurse practitioner, Angel, who recently had joined the Air Force and was discovering the discrepancy between what the recruiter had said and the actuality of life on the base. We were staying at a hotel and I wasn't feeling well; my pelvic area felt sore and I was uncomfortable. As the evening wore on, the pain in my abdomen continued to grow worse so I decided to take a hot bath. When the pain became unbearable, I woke Angel and said I needed to go to the emergency room now!

After sitting for what seemed like hours in the waiting room, I began to really feel what patients experience every day. Here I was, a health care professional, and I felt like a piece of worthless furniture, a nameless patient assigned a number and told to wait.

I was finally taken to an exam room, prodded and poked, and given two IV's, two pelvic exams; needles were thrust behind my cervix to see if there was any internal bleeding. The ER doctor thought I might have an ectopic pregnancy despite the fact that my husband had had a vasectomy. He didn't listen to me. Because the pain had dulled due to strong narcotics, they were about to send me

91

home when Angel, who became my advocate and guardian angel, pointed out that my abdomen was abnormally distended. I was so relieved that she spoke up. I had no connections at this hospital and didn't know any of the staff; I was really just a patient. Based on my distended abdomen, they took another blood test and found that my blood count had dropped dangerously low. I was then taken for an ultrasound. I remember being alone, covered with a sheet and in great pain. People were walking by but no one was listening, no one seemed to care. I felt abandoned, terrified; I remember screaming..."I'd rather have babies then deal with this pain!" Moments later the ultrasound technician took me, probably to shut me up, but I didn't care; the pain was beyond words. Next thing I knew I was being whisked into the operating room for emergency surgery. The surgeon began to tell me that I may lose my ovaries, my uterus or other organs and was attempting to get some kind of informed consent from me. I remember saying that I didn't care what he had to remove; I just wanted the pain to end.

I woke up hours later, alone, with no one to tell me why I had two new incisions on my stomach. In fact, no doctor or nurse ever told me what had transpired in the O.R. that night; it was the anesthesiologist who later checked on me because he was so alarmed during the procedure. He told me that when they opened me up, there was so much blood that I had to be given a blood transfusion, and they even had to call in the trauma unit. At one point, my blood pressure and heart rate dropped so low they had to give me atropine. The doctors thought they might lose me. The surgeon had suspected a ruptured ovary. Because of his sloppy performance, I still have a huge, zipper-like scar on my abdomen that goes all the way to just below my sternum. Perhaps this young resident-in-training didn't think about how a female patient may feel about her body upon recovery. It took a full year before I felt comfortable being naked around my husband. It is very disheartening for women to wake up from surgery feeling disfigured and mutilated.

As a health care provider, I knew what good nursing care was...the nursing care here was atrocious. No one helped me get up, no one helped me to the bathroom; no one even answered the call light! No one had brought me a meal in two days and the first meal they brought me was greasy pork chops and mashed potatoes. I knew if I ate this food it would cause blockages. I drank as many liquids as I could get my hands on and forced myself to get up and walk around so I could get the hell out of that hospital.

All of this happened on my birthday. My husband had intended to bring the kids down that weekend after the conference and we were all going to have fun on the beach. As it turned out, he wasn't there for me during this horrifying ordeal; he was back home with the kids and didn't know about the surgery until the next day. I felt abandoned. I felt so alone and wanted him simply to be there to hold my hand through those painful, scary times. However, he had his own set of problems to deal with; while playing at the beach, our middle child cut her foot on one of the toys and was rushed to the emergency room for stitches. Later, my husband and the children came for a visit and just seeing their beautiful faces warmed my heart and deepened my desire to leave the hospital.

I was finally discharged to home for further recovery. I did okay for a day. The second day home, the pain in my back and abdomen became unbearable, so I went to the local hospital. I was amazed that my colleagues didn't seem to realize the severity of my situation. I had to remind them that I just had an ovarian cyst rupture and lost two liters of blood! My concern was infection. An internist was consulted and they discovered that I had very enlarged lymph nodes along the aorta. One was preventing the kidney from draining. They also discovered an infection in my kidney. I was later informed that I would need to spend the night to determine if the kidney would drain on its own, or they would have to put in a stint, a tube to drain the kidney. My diagnosis was suspected cancer of the lymph nodes. The doctors were not optimistic about my condition.

A fellow friend and physician asked if there was anything he could do for me. I said, "yes, please go downstairs to my office and bring me my Bible from the top right hand drawer." He brought me the Bible and I spent the rest of the night focusing exclusively on Psalm 23, reading each line and meditating on the meaning of every word. Even though I felt alone and afraid, I knew God was with me. As I prayed, I asked God to protect me and keep me safe. I knew that whatever this was, lymphoma or kidney failure, I was going to be okay. I thought about my children and husband and felt such love for each one of them. As a mother and wife, I told God I wasn't ready to leave. My young children needed a mother to care for them and my husband needed a partner to raise them.

I didn't sleep all night. I guess I never understood what it was really like to feel like a helpless patient. I couldn't get up, I had no one to help me change my sweaty clothes as I broke through another round of frightening fevers and I had no one to share my concerns with. I just lay there feeling sweaty, scared and alone, but despite all that, I knew God was with me. I had faith.

After an endless night, I was wheeled to radiology to determine the status of my kidney. Thank God the kidney had drained and I was spared the stint. However, I was not spared from the bone marrow biopsy or the lymph node biopsy, which were both excruciating. Part of the frustration of being a patient is waiting for results. The surgeon who did the biopsy said my lymph nodes were "highly suspicious" and that he was almost positive that I had lymphoma. Had I believed him, I would have been thrown into a deep depression and weakened my immune system even further.

It took a full year to totally restore my health and get my energy level back. It was a year before I could wear pants that buttoned because of the pain from the scar on my abdomen. I was anemic due to all the blood loss. Because of blood transfusions and the threat of HIV infection, every six months for two years I had to be tested. A year later my lymph nodes had returned to normal size and all blockages had disappeared.

It is important to empower ourselves with the knowledge that we can heal. After all the tests, the diagnosis of lymphoma was removed. We still don't know what happened but I feel a miracle occurred between my prayers and beliefs and the prayers of others. Despite all the past pain and fear, I felt at peace. Part of that peace came from focusing on my children and my husband. When I looked at my loved ones and saw them growing up, or when I looked to the future and saw them graduating from high school, I knew I wanted to be there for all the milestones in their lives. I got out of my pain and sickness and got into my recovery and wellness. Focusing on others and taking my attention off the illness really helped me to get well. Love is very powerful. This whole experience served as a wake up call; it was a catalyst for my self-trans-formation. I had to re-direct my life. I had become so busy that I had lost sight of my own well-being. My illness allowed me to re-assess my life and try not to be everything to everybody but rather to be there for my family and myself. I now know that balance... time with family and time for myself...is critical to my well-being. I take time to honor my needs while still honoring the needs of others.

## Things I have learned through my journey to self-love:

1. Faith in God. Know that you don't need to have an intermediary to have a deep connection with God. Go to God with an open heart.

2. Some roads you have to travel alone. While others may influence you along the way, at the end of the day it is you and your Maker.

3. Love. Know that others love you and you love others and that the more you give, the more you get.

4. Balance is a life-long process so take time for yourself. Create mini-retreats, such as a massage, take a yoga class, exercise and meditate.

5. Journaling during times of distress helps lessen the crisis and helps to create clarity in a cluttered mind. If you want, throw it in the fire when you're done so you can burn the past.

6. Live your life with love and compassion. This is the corner-stone of my practice. Having experienced health care with different eyes, I am always there for my patients and when they are frightened, I comfort them. I remind them of their power within. Love is the best medicine.

Chapter 23

# SARAH'S JOURNEY
# From Passive to Proactive

## Sarah's Journal Entry, October 13, 1996

*I* feel so very alone right now! I have no one to talk with, no one to share my day's activities with...just no one at all. There is no one to understand my frustration with life in general...no one to share my day with. I am alone...so very alone...it is like coming home to an empty tunnel...(it is so sad to be alone in a world of so many people around you)...a tunnel that goes on and on and on. You can talk but no one lives here in a tunnel...your inner voice echoes into nothingness. I would rather be really alone than to be in a situation such as this...this is worse, much worse! There is a person around you but he does not hear, he doesn't feel, doesn't care. It is such a sad house...no joy, no feeling, no caring, no laughing, no smiling...no nothing...NOTHING...NOTHING AT ALL. I don't have to take this any more...I am a human being with lots of feeling and emotion and I am just so very tired of being pushed and jerked around by aggressive people who don't give a damn about anybody but themselves!

Being in a tunnel is so very unhealthy...I cannot breathe any-more, I cannot laugh...I cannot smile...the tunnel is so full of doom and sadness! It is pulling me down, down, down...the tunnel goes under the ground...under the world...under life...it is drowning me as though pulling me down into the depths of the ocean. This is the reverse of how I feel...water is so peaceful and I have this yearning to be by the water...but not in the tunnel...I have to get out...please God, let it be soon, or else I'll never come back. I can feel it...I am sinking daily in this tunnel of doom. I am so sad, so very sad...I can't seem to be able to surface...I am so very sad...please help me...I don't know where to turn. I am scared, I am lonely, I am unhappy...someone please help me...I am crying out for help...can't, someone help me...please...PLEASE, PLEASE!!!!!!"

My life began in 1941. Mom was delighted with the birth of a daughter, but not so for my dad; he wanted a boy. Much like other women born in my era, being a girl was not the easiest role to play. Fourteen months later my brother Mike was born and five years after that, my brother Josh came into the world. I was the eldest but dad rejected me because I was a girl...I felt very alienated from my father who made it painfully obvious that I was not wanted. Having sons, of course, fulfilled his wishes but the scars I had borne took years to erase.

Such were the beginnings of my feelings of passivity and alienation which would play out throughout my life until I began to see the effects of my belief systems on my present life. Out of necessity, mom worked evenings in a large department store and I began to dread nights because that is when it was obvious that I was ostracized. Dad was a "momma's boy"...the youngest of six kids who did not marry till he was thirty-nine years old. I also might add that his siblings broke off into two factions (two boys and one girl in each faction), and they did not get along. Every evening dad would talk to his mom (my grandmother) on the phone and tell her many untruths about my mother. I confided this information to her and needless to say, he changed the facts altogether, thus ostracizing me even more. In addition to this, dad drank a lot...as a child I was asked to go fetch him from the local bar and many nights a neighbor brought him home because dad couldn't find his way to our apartment...I was so embarrassed. Much of my early childhood is a blank, no conscious memory, and I feel this is from suppressing my unhappiness and rejection. I remember feeling insecure, abandoned, left and not loved by my dad. Fortunately, I did develop a close, loving relationship with my mother...she was my lifeline! She died suddenly at the age of 64 and it took me months to realize that I could not phone her any more and tell her all the news and events in my life.

I married the month after my twenty-first birthday...by today's standards and by my own realization, much too young. The first few years were fun and I was truly in love. I was a very meek, quiet child and this followed me into adulthood. Somewhere along the way I began to realize that I did not agree with or like a lot of my life anymore. I could not express this verbally...I just felt so lost and inadequate. I tried to talk to my husband Barry but to no avail. I resorted to writing letters to him...again, nothing. During this period of time we opened a business, which I ultimately ended up managing. This was the catalyst that made me a new person. I now had to make decisions by myself and I discovered that I was a good manager and smarter than I had given myself credit for. From our marriage I bore two wonderful sons and now I have two incredible grandchildren. Our marriage was no better but I had found a release. After some time, Barry found a part-time job in the evenings. It was a tremendous eye-opener to discover that I was finally free at home and I enjoyed this. I never understood that his constant controlling was engulfing me; I just did not realize it...all those years I never saw it but I just knew something was wrong. From that point on, I found my escape, our shop, and I thrived and the shop was a great success.

Fast forward about fourteen years...we sold our shop with plans to move South and start a new life...then the bomb fell. Barry's first love of his life, from some 28 years earlier, called out of the blue and entered his life. Chaos ensued. My life was shattered...my hopes to "start all over again" in a new place etc., were over. Through all this I still loved Barry. Events became worse and worse...like something out of a soap opera, the fighting, the drinking, the cheating, the lies, the deception...and so on. Even though we moved South, the affair continued. It was torture...it was hell...I was out of control with rage and jealousy. I began to smoke and drink heavily until I drank more and more. At my lowest point, I even considered suicide but somehow I could never execute a plan. Barry loves seductive women who dress and look this way. I tried that...I tried everything...nothing worked! During this time, the book, "Women Who Loved Too Much" by Robin Norwood became my lifeline. I devoured it! I still have it with all its underlined passages and many pages falling free and lots of tape holding it together. I couldn't sleep...friends were worried about me...I was a zombie...It was at a real low point in my life.

I went to a co-dependents anonymous group. Here I could pour out my heart and everyone listened. I attended the meetings for several months but then I realized that I was actually getting more depressed instead of better. I had heard about a stress/meditation group from a friend and figured it couldn't hurt; others seemed to be benefiting from it. I began attending a meditation for stress reduction group every Wednesday evening. I somehow felt more relaxed. To be honest, it was very difficult at first...my mind was all over the place and I had a hard time focusing, but I always felt better when I left. After about a year of attendance, I began to meditate daily. Oh what a difference that has made in my life! Meditation is essentially the way I start my day...for half an hour I am at complete peace! Sometimes I clear my mind completely; other times I talk to God about anything and everything. I have to say that meditation has changed my life...my thinking and my very way of being has changed in a way I never thought possible. It has now been three-and-a-half years since I first attended the meditation group and began deeply exploring my issues and rebuilding my self-esteem and taking my power back. I am now happy to say that I have left my marriage after 30 years and I am quite happy living on my own. I feel I have sprung wings and taken flight. I am now at peace with much in my present and have let go of much of my past. I have released the curse from my father and I now realize that this was what he knew at the time. It took much soul searching to produce this conclusion but I have reframed all the events in my childhood and have learned to extract the lessons learned and let the rest go. I am now free of dad's mark on my childhood.

Barry finally ended his relationship with his former sweetheart. He has never been able to say "I'm sorry...let's begin anew." He tried twice, once in the beginning and once four years later but never ended the affair. In fact, the affair continued unabated for seven years! Too much time had passed and I had grown both mentally and spiritually and knew I no longer had to stay in a dysfunctional marriage. I never left earlier because I wasn't ready and I was too scared. Now, I am so strong and I realize that Barry isn't a bad person, just not someone I wish to be around. He is everything I am not...bossy, negative, faultfinding and controlling. I also realize that I get along with everyone but Barry. I now know that he was always controlling me but until recently, I never saw it...I only knew that something was not right. Barry does not like the new me because I now refuse to be under his control; I am no longer under his power. I did not want to repeat the irony of my mother's passing just before she was to leave my father. I just turned 59 and have made up my mind to live the rest of my life in peace and serenity. I want it, I deserve it, and I am worthy of it! In fact, life is good...I find when I ask God for help He is always there for me. Sometimes answers come immediately and other times they take a little longer.

I am amazed that I often find the answer in one of my favorite books...I just open to any page and the answer is right there. Now, I don't even need to use a book, each day is an open dialogue with God and my higher self. My boys are successful in their careers and happily married. I am now in partnership with a wonderful friend in a business where my creativity blossoms. I still have to consciously re-program certain thoughts...I have a real problem with strong, aggressive and controlling people. They are my challenge but probably the wisest answer is to continue to stand in my power and remember that no one or nothing can affect me unless I let them. I have learned that you have to want to change...no one can do this for you. I also have to stop being the one to fix everything. Because I was such a shy, timid and meek child, Barry has always "teased" me because I was the perfect target. This is no longer true...I will no longer let it happen. I always remember a child's book, "Never tease a weasel...teasing is not nice," which we read to our boys as they grew up. Teasing is cruel...hurting at someone else's expense for a laugh is not kind.

Life is now great. Contentment and peace surround me...I am finally happy. I also know that I must constantly be aware...it is easy to fall back into old habits. My daily meditation is my lifesaver; the serenity and peace I find in meditation is beyond words. For 30 minutes every morning I am mindful of absolutely nothing and it is glorious. Other times I sometimes work out problems peacefully and the answers always come. I am on my way...I have come so far...the obsession of my relationship with Barry, the pleaser and the nice girl...my, my, my how my life has changed.

## Sarah's Top Five Strategies for Self-Transformation:

1. Daily practice of meditation for 30 minutes each morning

2. Self acceptance and acceptance of others

3. Positive Affirmations/Journaling

4. Volunteering (Twice a week she picks up bread and cakes from two local grocers and brings them to organizations that help the community and feed the poor.) Love is service in action!

5. Belief in self, self-confidence and a deep inner strength.

# CHAPTER 24

# JOANNA'S STORY
## Finding Family and Discovering Self

**W**ho am I? Beyond all the things I say or have; who am I? What are the qualities of my nature or being that uniquely describe me, truly define me? Are these special elements best reflected in the essence of my spirit or the motion of my heart? For me trying to grasp this knowingness has been like dancing with my shadow. When I think I have it, it disappears or moves away from my reach, that is until a few years ago when I got the answer I was seeking.

### Closing the Baltic Circle

My father was born in 1918 in Wisconsin and grew up in a small town on the shores of Lake Michigan. The youngest son of Lithuanian immigrant parents, he was a handsome, lean and athletic young man and was the "baby" of the family, with four older siblings. My father's oldest brother and first-born of the siblings was my Uncle Stasys, an uncle I never met. An uncle whose fate was to remain in Lithuania all his days on earth.

My grandparents, Joseph and Mary, left Lithuania in the early 1900's for a better life and in pursuit of the American Dream. Upon embarkation at the passenger ship, they were told by authorities that their first-born son and only child at the time, Stasys, approximately six years old, could not travel with them on the ship because of an eye infection. This twist of fate changed the course of their lives forever. Heart-wrenching, yet with courage beyond comprehension, they were determined to set out on their journey to America with full intention to send for little Stasys later. Stasys remained under the care of his aunt in Lithuania. After my grandparents arrived in the United States, economic times became difficult, settling into life in America, speaking a foreign language and then, before long, seeing the wall that was to become the Iron Curtain begin to take shape...the wall that kept Stasys from the arms of his parents.

Little Stasys had been left behind, leaving a large hole in the family circle. A sadness so deep in a country so torn by destruction. He would never see his parents again, never meet his younger sisters Mary, Anne and Veronica, all born in Wisconsin, and never bond with his baby brother Peter. Stasys passed from this earth at the age of 87. Like me, he was raised in the protective circle of extended family. After much divine searching, I can now see that Stasys and I share a similar thread in our lives, that of being left behind as young children in a confusing world of wonder and loss.

My mother died shortly after I was born. It was a complicated birth with her second child, a daughter, and in the day that followed this birthing she sadly lost too much blood during the difficult delivery. Lorraine died at 28 years young. I was 18 months old and unaware of the big hole in my heart that would soon grow. A striking dark-haired, brown-eyed beauty, whom I know only through black and white photos and the stories I heard throughout my life.

My mom fell in love with and married a handsome young private first-class World War II veteran, named Peter. They were a striking couple – her dark-haired beauty and his blonde chiseled Baltic features. Like many immigrant families of the early 1900's, Peter's parents had changed their last name from the original Lithuanian surname. Was it because of the immensity of Ellis Island processing, language barrier misunderstandings or simply not realizing what had translated before them? I will never know the true reason.

A young woman's death is a sad affair, but a mother dying in childbirth, well, what could be worse? Leaving behind a young daughter and the love of a husband is a sadness that lasts a lifetime. While my mother's death was tragic, I was fortunate. There was some light. Two great loving and giving women came to my rescue - my Aunts Mary and Anne, sisters to my father, Lights of God to me. After my mother died, my father and I lived with Aunt Mary and her husband and they assumed the duties as my day-to-day care givers. Aunt Mary became my 'mom'. She washed me, fed me, played with me, took me to church every Sunday and held me safe until my father returned home from work each day. She did this unconditionally for three years until my father married Nora a few years later. Nora was a brave soul to take on a husband and a daughter. Being a devoted Catholic, she completed her sacred vigils to ensure that this was the right decision for her. She gave her caring and love unconditionally in her new role as mom/stepmom.

Aunt Mary was devoted to her "little brother" Pete and devoted to me. But her love did not stop there. Mary could love in that big way that only close families are able to witness and celebrate. She carried enough love to care for her own child and the 17 nieces and nephews who were to follow. I guess you could say I grew up in a crowd of family and because of this I did not have much opportunity to feel lonely. I was loved by all, but different. In a sea of fair skinned blondes, I was, like my mother, of olive complexion, brunette and brown-eyed. Mary, knowing this or sensing this, always had a special place in her heart for me. She just knew I needed special care, not in big obvious ways, but through a language I wasn't even aware of. She knew that while my mother did not intend to leave me behind, I would forever be without the strong bond of a mother-daughter relationship...a piece of me that I could never visually see...a part that I know I longed for.

During the time after my mother's death and quietly throughout my life there has been another angel, my father's sister, Anne, but after Mary's passing, Anne became even closer to my father until she died at 84 years of age. She was a woman of few words...strong, articulate and vibrant. She worked tirelessly raising seven children of her own. She never missed a day when she did not call my father to "check in." Their daily chats were nothing like today's true confessions or existential examinations of "how life was treating me," but just to make sure everything was going okay. That was it, okay. They just wanted to make sure one or the other didn't need anything. My father and his sisters were from the "don't complain about life school of living." They just did what they had to do and loved each other strongly from a somewhat unspoken distance. Actions spoke louder than words for my father's generation.

Like my father and Mary, Anne loved all that came from her family and would do anything for them. She wrote me letters about my mother and shared warm stories about her. Another older sister, named Veronica, was part of this circle of love. Veronica and her family lived close by and were always part of the family gatherings until Veronica passed away in her forties from cancer. There was never a party or a special occasion that the three siblings and their herd of children didn't get together. Easter, Thanksgiving, birthdays, communions, summer picnics and vacations in Door County; each occasion was a time for joyous family togetherness and for each of my 17 cousins and me to grow close and create a circle that would last a lifetime.

Like Mary, Veronica could sense what it must feel like to be left behind. In a crowd of cousins, I stood out, looking like Annette Funicello in a crowd of blonde haired, blued-eyed Baltics, but they just kept bringing me in the circle with their love. How can one resist? Yet, despite the wonders of my father, the love of his sisters and the love of my cousins, I still wondered – who am I really? Where do I fit in? I felt different.

Over the years Anne, Mary and Veronica would often write their brother in Lithuania, sending him money, clothes and household items they thought he might need. I recall a story about the FBI interviewing Aunt Mary and putting her name on a so-called "list" of Americans to be watched who were communicating with family under Soviet occupation. Why? Her love was wider than the whole Soviet Union. Nothing could stop her from sending sewing machine parts to brother Stasys. He was a tailor and this was his livelihood. I remember hearing my Aunt Mary speaking with her sister in Lithuanian or speaking with my grandparents in the native tongue. I guess none of us paid much attention to the fact that we had an uncle and three cousins in a foreign land. We were too busy and focused on our lives to be concerned with people we had never met who lived in a country we knew nothing about. I guess like all kids we just figured our folks would take care of maintaining the family ties – we had our own lives to live. That was then.

Fast forward to a day in 1998. I was in my late 40's, visiting with my father. We had received some sporadic letters over the years from Uncle Stasys's daughter, my cousin Ona, in Lithuania. I, personally, had never directly communicated with Ona, but it seemed at this visit my father was handing over the "pen and paper" to me. He asked that I write a letter to the Lithuanian family. After all, it was getting close to Christmas and dear Dad always seemed to find a few extra American $100's to send to our Lithuanian family. Perhaps he was "engaging" me into the circle in his own unspoken way.

As I look back on that day and that simple conversation, I wonder about the moments in life that forever change us. Many times they are not ones filled with great sorrow, joy or achievement, but quiet little shudders in time that seem to move us in a new direction. If we listen, these moments are like oracles that whisper and bid us to come further and look deeper.

So, I wrote my first letter to my Lithuanian cousin Ona and thereby, somewhat unknowingly, picked up the torch that my aunts had carried before me during their lifetimes. I wrote a humble letter of introduction. (I should know these family members better. My God, they are my first cousins!) This is your cousin Joanna, and this is a short version of my life and my daughter's life. How are you? Tell me about your life. Your joys. Your hardships. I look forward to hearing all about you.

What ensued was magic! Ona's reply simply stated, among other things, "please come to visit us and your homeland. Our country is independent again and many Americans are now visiting. We will take good care of you and show you our small, but beautiful Lithuania." I remember sitting at my kitchen table reading the letter to my daughter and feeling Ona's warmth and sincerity tingle up my spine. I looked at my daughter, Kelly, and said, "we have to go!" Another quiet shudder in time. There was no turning back! This was now my mission. Somehow, someway, I was going. I rallied my sisters, brothers and cousins to this idea, and after many discussions and one year's worth of planning and saving, we departed in a mighty group of nine family members to spend 10 days in our homeland, a country we knew little about and an adventure we anticipated with enthusiasm.

Upon arrival at the Vilnius airport, we felt heightened anticipation in coming face to face with our first cousins. Could there even be family resemblances? We were sure of it from the few pictures we received over the years. It was a moment, and this time, a loud shudder of joy that trembled through my body. Hugging cousin Ona, who had kept the dream alive of seeing her American family, was a complete outpouring of emotion filled with tremendous spirit and love. This was, after all, almost 80 years of family disconnection being restored in that incredible moment of first reunion. A moment that our Lithuanian cousins could only dream about during their lifetime. What followed in the days ahead were special moments of traditional toasts with rye bread and vodka, welcome dinner at Ona's house, testimonials from cousins Algis and Irena about their father's dream of seeing his American family, seeing the farm fields where my grandparents lived before they left Lithuania and picking some wheat growing in these fields to take a piece of that history home with us. We toured this charming country and saw the beauty of the Baltic Sea, the sadness in the people's faces, but also felt the energy of being "home" again. There is incredible spirit in finding disconnected family – of going back to your roots, a healing. A closing of the circle. A broken circle that no longer has to endure pain. A knowing that you had help from higher sources. God's hand. Aunt Mary's spirit. Aunt Anne's strength. Uncle Stasys' dream. They all played significant roles in the spiritual realm, always guiding us along this reunion journey. As my father said, "your generation could finally do what ours could not...go with freedom to meet, explore and know each other."

So, my searching of "who am I," "why do I feel different" flourishes with renewed love and reconnection to this Baltic family I identify so closely with. From all things that, at first, appear confusing, painful or unfair, there is wonderful opportunity if we are patient and listen and follow the clues and whispers of life. Perhaps it was my mother dying when I was so young and me being "left behind" as Stasys was "left behind" that has turned me into a searcher of sorts and led me to this family reconnection. We often make too much out of life's seeming disappointments or failures, but if we could see the meaning of things, we would celebrate these moments as gifts from God and pathways to ourselves.

My journey continues and will always be a work in progress. Isn't that our mission? To be the best we can be. I will listen more carefully and follow the clues and whispers and soft shudders as they come into my life. And forever celebrate our family circle in its completeness!

### Joanna's Tools for Transformation:
1. Intuition. Listen to it. Pay attention to it. It guides you.
2. Be patient in life. Follow clues in your life for wonderful opportunities.
3. Meditation. Be quiet and still. Hear the whispers.
4. Stay focused. Persevere through life's challenges. You will grow from them.
5. Love openly. Do not fear its strength.

Section III

# Tools for
# Self-Transformation

*"Man did not weave the Web of life,*
*he is merely a strand in it.*
*Whatever he does to the Web,*
*he does to himself."*

CHIEF SEATTLE

CHAPTER 25

# Rekindling the Need for Rituals

*I*ndigenous cultures the world over have some form of ritual, ceremonies to celebrate life's passages. Rites of passage are sorely lacking in our modern, technological, fast-paced culture. We long for a deeper connection with the Earth, each other and our own sacred selves. In our search for harmony and meaning in a seemingly meaningless world, we need rituals to restore our spirit and keep us close to what is real.

Personal rituals restore a sense of sacredness to our lives. They keep us grounded in the here and now. I have created a special place in my home for meditation and yoga, a space filled with candles, incense from India and a meditation cushion. I choose peaceful music specifically designed for meditation and relaxation, and I employ toning bells, Tibetan singing bowls and a large gong. These tools transform me and create that sacred space which feeds my body, mind and spirit. This sanctuary brings a feeling of reverence to both my practice and my life.

Another of my personal rituals is yoga. I spread out my sticky mat and begin to focus on my breathing. I also take this time to set the intent for the rest of the day. Often accompanied by my yoga teacher (my husband), I do a series of poses that tone my body, strengthen and stimulate my immune system and quiet my active mind.

Another of my rituals is soaking in a hot tub with lavender bath salts or other therapeutic, aromatic additions. Soaking in the tub becomes another form of meditation or inner communion. As the jets stimulate my body and the warm water soothes my tired muscles, my spirit takes flight and I feel free of worldly distractions.

Personal rituals are an integral part of our total well-being. Think of ways to bring a feeling of sacredness back into your life. A drumming circle by a roaring fire evokes a profound cellular memory of an ancient past and a simpler time. A tribal dance

releases the shaman within and allows us to free our spirit through a trance-like dance. A re-occurring theme in my work with women at wellness retreats is the power of movement. Deep down we all love to dance, to move our bodies and be free! We yearn for total liberation from earthly restraints; tribal dancing creates a space for just that. When we dance with our eyes closed and go within, a whole new world opens to us...when we let go and become totally unaffected by external factors, the soul soars and our bodies follow suit. The dance becomes you and you become the dance. The dance represents life itself, each movement taking us deeper into our true self, our unbridled wild selves. Rituals such as trance/tribal dancing allow us to heal the rift between body and mind, to end the dichotomy between soul and matter and to re-connect us to our wholeness. Our bodies move beyond normal reality, akin to ancient experiences of the evolution of our consciousness.

Native Americans embodied complete comprehension of the power of rituals and honoring the sacredness of all life. To the Ancient Ones, or Anasazi, spirituality and nature were inextricably intertwined. They saw the physical world as a reflection of the spiritual world. Native Americans understand the symbiotic relationship with nature, especially plants and animals. They honor all life.

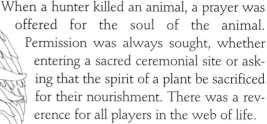

When a hunter killed an animal, a prayer was offered for the soul of the animal. Permission was always sought, whether entering a sacred ceremonial site or asking that the spirit of a plant be sacrificed for their nourishment. There was a reverence for all players in the web of life.

Modern life has torn the delicate web that connected us with nature. It is this symbiotic relationship that has been lacerated by the "civilized" world. We need to be more conscious of our connection to Mother Earth. We need to tread lightly and honor all life forms.

As we rekindle the sense of magic and ritual in our lives, let us remember the purpose of these ceremonies...to keep us close to what is real and sacred and to remind us that we are all inner-connected to the great dance of life.

## Exploratory Questions for Rekindling the Need for Rituals

1. What rituals do I practice that keep me in balance?
2. When was the last time I gave myself permission to take a long, hot bath complete with candles and bath salts and really pampered myself?
3. How long has it been since I really let loose and did some form of expressive dance?
4. When was the last time I sang from the bottom of my heart at the top of my lungs?
5. Am I inspired to create a sacred space to center my mind and balance my life?
6. Do I honor all life and am I willing to be a good steward of Mother Earth?

# CHAPTER 26

# Journaling from the Heart

**W**riting down your thoughts, or journaling, is a powerful tool for self-transformation. View journaling as a journey to wholeness, a roadmap that details your quest to find the elusive self. "Wide open" journaling allows for the release of pent up emotions and unexpressed anger. You could equate journaling to a mind dump; it is like a healing crisis via the pen. There are many ways to express your truth. Writing your feelings down on paper in a "stream of consciousness" fashion allows you to sidestep the intellect and release. With journaling, anything goes and everything written helps to let go. Journaling generates many benefits in addition to emotional catharsis. Psychologist James Pennebaker, a professor at Southern Methodist University in Dallas, ushered groups through a journaling exercise, asking participants to write about their most traumatic experience for 20 minutes on four consecutive days. His research repeatedly demonstrated remarkable benefits derived from writing about traumatic events. Participants not only felt better emotionally but their physical health improved as well. Compared to control groups who wrote about trivial events, the "journalists" made significantly fewer visits to the doctor and reported less symptoms of illness for months after the study. Pennebaker and his colleagues also found that certain key immune cells were livelier for weeks following the experiment. Many of us have experienced devastating traumas that we've never disclosed to others. Cindy, a 38-year-old client of mine, was only recently able to journal and disclose the horror of being sexually abused by

> *"Be patient toward all that is unsolved in your heart and try to love the questions themselves...Do not now seek the answers which cannot be given you because you would not be able to live them and the point is to live everything. Live the questions now. Perhaps you will then gradually, without noticing it, live along some distant day into the answer."*
>
> RAINER MARIA RILKE,
> LETTERS TO A YOUNG POET

her grandfather for the first 11 years of her life. The abuse stopped at age 11 with her grandfather's death. It seemed that by not sharing her deep trauma, shame, and guilt, Cindy developed a whole host of physical problems throughout her life. She became ill with Crohn's disease, an inflammation of the intestines that often results in chronic vomiting, diarrhea, cramps, weight loss and internal bleeding. Unresolved issues and pain manifested internally. She felt like she could no longer "stomach the world." Journaling, along with other release work, allowed her to recognize her body's way of expressing the buried pain, sorrow and anger that was eating away at her internally. She felt that her physical self was out of control and this emotional act of writing stimulated the part of her that most needed to be healed. Her physical problems led her to do some exploratory surgery of the soul, journaling and recalling wounds long buried. She's begun to fully heal and many of her symptoms have disappeared.

Now that you know the benefits of journaling, let's explore how to do it. There is no right or wrong way; simply let your thoughts and feelings flow freely and uncensored. Turn the literary critic off and let your inner voice surface. Write words, phrases, thoughts or sentences, use whatever method works for you. Journal about a particular feeling or event.

## Here are some topics to get you going, to spark your inner poet:

Breaking Open to Love
Pausing In the Stillness
The Dance of Life
The Struggle to Know
Coming Home
Being In my Center
Letting Go of Fear
Opening to the Mystery
Spiraling Through
Moving My Body
Clinging to: ─────────────
Pushed and Pulled by: ──────────

Journey to: ──────────────────

These topics can serve as a vehicle for your inner poet. Allow the many questions that pull your intellect to be answered from within.

# *If I Had My Life To Live Over*

*If I had my life to live over, I'd like to make more
    mistakes next time.
I would limber up.
I would be sillier than I have been this trip.
I would take fewer things seriously.
I would take more chances.
I would climb more mountains and swim more
    rivers.
I would eat more ice cream and less beans.
I would perhaps have more actual troubles,
but I'd have fewer imaginary ones.
You see, I'm one of those people who live sensibly and
    sanely hour after hour, day after day.
Oh, I've had my moments, and if I had it to do over
    again, I'd have more of them!
In fact, I'd try to have nothing else.
Just moments, one after another instead of living so
    many years ahead of each day.
I've been one of those persons who never goes any-
    where without a thermometer,
    a hot water bottle, a raincoat, and a parachute.
If I had it to do over again, I would travel lighter
    than I have.
If I had my life to live over, I would start barefoot
    earlier in the Spring and
    stay that way later in the Fall.
I would go to more dances.
I would ride more merry-go-rounds.
I would pick more daisies.*

FROM THE JOURNAL OF NADINE STAIR, AGE 85

Chapter 27

# The Benefits of Bodywork & Massage

We all need to be touched. The skin is the largest sensory organ and touch is one of the greatest senses we possess. We learn about touch the moment we are born. Each of us defines touch differently but, without a doubt, touch is a necessary ingredient in optimal wellness. Bodywork is a powerful tool for both touch and therapeutic healing. Bodywork is defined as the application of touch by one person to another, to produce relaxation, pain relief, injury rehabilitation, health improvement, increased awareness, emotional release or pleasure. The term massage usually refers to the traditional Swedish massage characterized by the five strokes; effleurage (stroking), petrissage (kneading), friction, vibration and tapotement (tapping). Massage, an ancient art, is having a renaissance. During the last fifty years, many new types of massage have been developed which have a multitude of benefits.

*"By releasing the chronically held traumas of a lifetime and reconnecting the natural flows and balances of the organism, the Rolf system seeks to increase health and vitality, to alleviate stress and tension, and to encourage growth and openness on all levels of organismic functioning".*
KEN DYCHTWALD

Massage increases circulation, reduces muscle tension, strengthens the immune system and restores balance to the nervous, limbic and endocrine systems. Massage is excellent for infants, children, adolescents, adults and older adults...the whole age continuum benefits from bodywork and massage.

Body/mind therapies are especially helpful for the exploratory surgeon in facilitating the release of emotional blocks in the body. One such therapeutic intervention is Rolfing, a system developed by the late Dr. Ida Rolf which involves deep massage to unlock muscle tension and tightness and elicit fascial release. This in turn releases pent-up emotions.

For many people, receiving bodywork by trained professionals is the only time they are touched. Many people live alone and therefore do not often get touched or enjoy the daily benefits of

"Vitamin T" (a phrase coined by colleague Bob Czimbal signifying Vitamin Touch). According to Czimbal, having a full-body massage gives you a megadose of Vitamin T.

A plethora of different types of bodywork and massage techniques exist. The subject is too vast to explore in this book, but I will share a few of the top bodywork modalities whose therapeutic benefits warrant further exploration:

● Sports massage – for training, preparation and recovery from exertion during sporting events. (Notice how almost every sports team and Olympic team has a sports massage therapist on staff.)

● Wellness massage – massage for preventive measures and also to relieve daily stressors and maintain good muscle tone.

● Rehabilitative massage – for recovery after physical injury such as broken bones.

● Neuromuscular massage – designed to work with the nervous system and muscular system to facilitate a release of muscular tension and to stretch and lengthen muscles and connective tissue.

● Therapeutic Touch/Reiki – Energetic approaches which work on aligning the energy systems in the body with light touch.

● Reflexology - involves stimulating reflex points on the feet, hands or ears, which in turn restores balance to the entire body.

● Yoga – A body/mind technique that employs both physical postures along with meditation practices.

The benefits of bodywork and massage cannot be underestimated on the journey to self-love. Simply by utilizing some of these techniques you gain a greater appreciation for your body and mind. Furthermore, bodywork allows for the release of physical and emotional blocks that can keep you from full consciousness.

## Exploratory Questions for the Benefits of Bodywork & Massage

1. Do you receive regular bodywork or massage?
2. When was the last time you had a full body massage or have you ever had a massage?
3. In what ways do you give and receive "Vitamin T?"
4. Are you willing to explore different body/mind techniques that you may not be familiar with?

CHAPTER 28

# YOGA

**Y**oga is an ancient science of bringing harmony between the body and the mind. Yoga has been around for thousands of years.

Yoga is sometimes defined as a union, a coming together. This union can be interpreted to mean the body and mind, the physical and spiritual, or even the mental and emotional. There are various definitions and varieties of yoga. One of the most popular and well-known forms of yoga is Hatha Yoga. Hatha is defined as Sun and Moon, hence a union between two forces. This form of yoga involves breathing, concentration, focus and certain body positions. The practice of these postures combined with the breathing brings about relaxation, increased flexibility and strength, improved balance, increased lung capacity, increased blood flow to the internal organs, lowered blood pressure, and even a certain blissfulness.

*"Yoga is for everyone, for the West as well as the East. One would not say the telephone is not for the East because it was invented in the West. Through yoga, we can build a direct line to God."*
YOGANANDA

Yoga has helped me overcome an old shoulder injury. I've gone from being unable to lift 10 pounds over my head to doing handstands. There are classes now available all over the country in churches, YMCA's, schools, homes, recreation centers, senior centers, even the Yellow Pages. There are more and more studies showing the benefits of practicing yoga for all age groups; it's never too late to begin. Before you start, however, call and talk to the instructor, get a feel for his or her personality and see if it suits yours. Ask if you could watch a portion of the class before you sign up; get a feel to make sure you're going to experience the type of yoga class you're looking for. There are usually some guidelines the teacher may inform you of pertaining to the classes; respect and honor them. Inform the teacher of any injuries, even get your doctor's okay if you're not sure about your health. Be patient with your body, especially if you've had injuries or you are not very flexible. After all, it's taken you years to get stiff! Have fun with your practice, be creative, explore your body and re-acquaint

"Blessed are the flexible, for they shall not be bent out of shape."

ANONYMOUS

yourself with it. Know that some days your body will be very responsive and other days it can be just as stubborn as we ourselves are. Make your practice a sacred time. Create a place in your home if you can't find a class, get a book or a video, and use it as your teacher. Be committed. Results happen when the dedication is there. Honor and respect your body and don't force things to happen. Be gentle. Yoga can and will affect your life in many ways – physically, emotionally, mentally and spiritually. Remember, yoga is not about trying to put both feet behind your head, but to keep a peace of mind no matter what you are doing. One of my teachers would say "just because you can bring your head to the floor or put both feet behind your head doesn't make you more enlightened than someone who can't."

Let's take a moment to try a simple practice. Lie on your back, relax your torso, and feel the back of your neck and head sinking into the floor. Pull your right knee into your chest and keep the left leg extended on the floor. Wrap you hands below the right knee and gently press your knee into your hands. This stretch helps tight lower back muscles relax. Stay as long as you like. Then slowly release and change sides.

Another great stretch to strengthen and stretch the back is to come onto your hands and knees, like a table, keeping the palms flat and under the shoulders. Try to keep the arms straight. Open the knees hip width apart. Now as you inhale, lift the chest away from the floor, look forward and lift the tailbone to the ceiling. As you exhale, tuck your tailbone down toward the floor, round the back and drop your chin into the chest. This is called the cat and cow pose. If you need to use a blanket under the knees, do so. If your wrists are  tight, try coming onto your forearms and see how that feels. Listen to and observe your body and what goes on as you move. Take your time and move slowly. Let go of your fears and inhibitions. Try some yoga today and let the transformation begin.

117

CHAPTER 29

# Why Diets Don't Work

*I*n the past 20 years the incidence of eating disorders such as bulimia and anorexia, chronic dieting, and exercise addictions has risen dramatically. Studies indicate this is directly related to unhealthy media messages. Models today, for example, weigh 25 percent less than they did several decades ago, and their photos are repeatedly re-touched for perfection. Most of these models are between the ages of 15 to 19, with the exception of a few super-models who have maintained longer careers. An adolescent body is quite different from an adult body. If you need a reminder, check your high school graduation picture. Our bodies change over time and look quite different at 15 than at 30...a natural process.

Society's answer to weight problems has been diets – carbo diets, protein diets, juicing diets – you name it, it's out there. But diets do not work. Instead they can compound the problem of weight loss! Ample data suggests dieting can cause eating disorders, problematic eating and even lead to weight gain – more than 90 percent of all dieters regain more weight than they originally lost within a three-year follow-up period. Studies show diets may actually increase a person's risk for heart disease because of the roller coaster effect on the body. Other studies reveal that for every diet there is an equal and opposite binge; like cause and effect, every action has a reaction.

Physiologically, dieting is hard on the body and can have damaging effects on the metabolism. Reduced calorie intake and frequent dieting actually slows the metabolic rate, which makes the body very effective at storing food. It perceives the dieter is in lean times and will store the food as fat to ensure there are reserves within the body. Many women who say they only eat once a day or eat very little have a hard time losing weight because the body may be trying to conserve what they are eating. If there is little or no exercise, the food will be stored as fat. It is actually better to eat more food throughout the day to keep the metabolism going, like keeping a fire stoked with wood to burn as fuel. Keep the fire burning with regular, smaller meals versus eating once a day.

Well women (and men) don't diet because they love themselves unconditionally and choose foods that support their health and well-being. They don't obsess about every calorie consumed or every gram of fat digested.

What well women and men do instead is adopt a wellness lifestyle based on healthy eating habits, moderate exercise and positive behaviors that support their well-being. New research shows the physical and emotional benefits of *moderate, enjoyable* exercise.

Formerly, when I worked at a health education center and taught prevention classes, the old prescription for exercise was 30 to 60 minutes of continuous, vigorous exercise 3 to 5 times a week. The newer, saner prescription calls for moderate exercise that includes everything from gardening to grocery shopping and walking to washing the car. Researchers have found that accumulated periods of exercise or physical activity such as walking up a flight of stairs or walking down a long driveway to the mailbox are probably equivalent to a vigorous workout like aerobics. And don't forget about burning calories and toning muscles on the dance floor! Another study demonstrated how people who exercise in short spurts actually seem to get a greater boost in their ratio of HDL or "good" cholesterol to LDL or "bad" cholesterol. Every little bit of exercise counts.

## The Benefits of Moderate, Joyful Exercise are:

- Reducing the risk of heart disease and stroke
- Increasing confidence and self-esteem
- Improving mood and increasing the secretion of endorphins
- Boosting immunity
- Raising HDL or "good" cholesterol in the blood stream
- Decreasing stress and anxiety
- Strengthening muscles and building strong bones
- Helping maintain *your* healthy body weight
- Reducing high blood pressure over time

Wellness is not a fad anymore than healthy eating or positive thinking is. Wellness is a way of life, it is a life-long journey to wholeness and if we can begin to see our body, mind and spirit as wonderful tools for self-transformation, self-love and self mastery will surely follow.

## *Exploratory Questions for Why Diets Don't Work*

1. Do I try every new diet to no avail?
2. Am I trying to meet society's standard of what a healthy weight is?
3. Am I starving myself in the morning and grazing in the evening?
4. Have I adopted a moderate exercise program that I love?
5. What fun physical activities can I engage in that will be both mentally satisfying and physically rewarding?

# CHAPTER 30

# Diet and Nutrition

$S$ince this is not a book on nutrition, I will not spend a lot of time on this subject as the tool kit is designed to have quick tips to transform. There are a plethora of books on the subject of nutrition and I would strongly suggest that you read those that resonate with you. Here are a few basic recommendations to keep you well on your way to self mastery.

## Healthy Eating

For healthy eating, it is usually best to stop dieting and learn how to respond to your true hunger signals. Eat when you are hungry and stop when you are full. Don't reach for food out of boredom or a need for comfort. We are usually propelled to the pantry when we feel tired or angry.

## Tips for taming hunger:

- Drink a glass of water. Much of our hunger pangs stem from dehydration, so drink ample amounts of purified water.
- Take a walk or climb stairs when you begin to feel anxious and want to grab the closest bag of cookies or chips.
- Keep yourself busy with other activities that are life affirming - like spending time with a good friend or a new hobby.
- When you are tired and over-extended, comfort food is what you want. However, the better choice may be a nap or a brisk walk in fresh air, or curling up with a good book.

It is important to eat a variety of foods from all the different food groups. The typical American diet centers around meats, sugars, and fats, which do not contain enough fiber. Studies show an increased incidence of breast, colon and other cancers with a high meat intake. Add more fiber to your diet; "roughage" helps maintain a healthy weight and a clean colon. Fiber also promotes cholesterol clearance from the blood thereby reducing the risk of heart disease. An easy way to add fiber to your diet is through fruit. For example, have an apple instead of apple pie, choose fresh fruit for dessert. The other benefits of fruits and vegetables are their high water content which fills you up without filling you out. Adopt a more plant-based diet and get plenty of soy in the form of soy milk, tofu or other forms – soy protein is a good source of phytoestrogens, which assist in building strong bones and aid in easing some of the discomfort associated with menopause.

Eat more grains such as whole wheat, brown rice, cereals, pasta and multi-grain breads. According to the new food pyramid, 60 percent of your total calories (6-11 servings) should come from whole grains, cereals, pasta, and bread. Include three to five servings of fresh vegetables and two to four servings of fresh fruits in your daily diet. Choose to bake, broil, saute, steam or stir-fry your cooked foods rather than frying. Opt for low-fat dairy products, especially yogurt that has not been treated with hormones. Better yet, try to adopt a pre-industrial diet based on whole foods that come "all natural." The bulk of the American diet consists of food that is packaged, processed and highly refined. Much of it is canned, frozen, preserved, enriched and now genetically altered. You may not be aware of the hormones, pesticide residues, antibiotics and other things in your food! We need to revisit our eating habits and food production methods, living closer to the land and in harmony with Mother Nature, not as adversaries polluting the Earth and ourselves.

You don't have to go without; simply choose healthier options. You can have your cake and eat it too, just use whole wheat flour instead of white! Remember, food is not the enemy. Food is to be enjoyed, celebrated and integrated into a healthy lifestyle. Make the dinner table a celebration of life, not a battlefield.

## Exploratory Questions for Diet and Nutrition

1. Am I eating a variety of foods from all food groups?
2. Do I drink at least 8 glasses of water a day?
3. How can I get more fiber in my diet?
4. Do I eat organic produce when I can?
5. Have I created a garden to grow herbs for cooking?
6. Do I enjoy my food? Is every meal a celebration?

# CHAPTER 31

# Ten Top Strategies for Total Well-Being

1. Visualize yourself as the embodiment of wellness; see yourself as strong, whole and happy.

2. See your body, mind and spirit as healthy and when you feel vulnerable, weak or self-conscious, simply remind yourself that you are beautiful just the way you are.

3. Choose foods that are nutritious, life supporting and enjoyable. Be mindful of the way you eat and take time to chew your food, appreciate the flavors, the textures and the quality of your food. Rather than feeling you have to give up what you love, choose healthier options.

4. Choose an exercise that is enjoyable to you; seek to find ways to move your body that are pleasurable for you. Aerobics may not be for everyone, but perhaps you like to swim, dance, do yoga, tai chi, or garden; all are fine, what is important is that you do what you love.

5. Choose to have loving, supportive friendships, colleagues, partners and family members. Remind yourself that no one or nothing can affect you unless you let them. Remember that you have choices about who you spend your time with.

6. Take quality time for yourself where no one can disturb your peace, as often as you can. If possible, spend 10 to 15 minutes daily for self-reflection and renewal. Remind yourself that you deserve it, and remember if you don't go within, you go without.

7. Remember to keep a sense of humor. Make a promise to fill your life with purpose, passion, love and laughter.

8. Focus on the positive, not the negative. See the best in yourself and others. Rather than being quick to judge, be quick to praise. Focus on what you want, not what you don't want.

9. Take time to feed the spirit through reconnecting with nature, being with loved ones, deepening your spirituality, meditating, listening to music that uplifts you; whatever it is that touches your heart and makes your soul sing...*do it.*

10. Have a deep reverence for all the world's well-being. Realize we are all interconnected.

CHAPTER 32

# The Art of Meditation and Deep Relaxation

*T*here are multiple styles of meditation and many different approaches but the ultimate goal is the same...achieving peace of mind. Meditation means many things to different people. For me, meditation has become a profound spiritual practice and a life-saving stress reduction technique. Meditation is the art of focusing your attention so completely on your inner dialogue that you detach from everything else around you. This inner dialogue is then finely tuned so that you may play the instrument of your mind in flawless precision. Thoughts begin to flow, leading to a stream of consciousness that becomes a still pool of inner reflection. Stillness is best achieved by focusing on a few key words such as peace, love, Om, Shalom, God or affirmations such as "I am a peaceful soul." The phrase "Om Shanti" or "I am a peaceful soul" is often repeated in India, in meditation. It is an empowering statement for transformation.

Of all the tools in the exploratory surgeon's kit, meditation is the most life altering. This is where the real laboratory lies, where thoughts are centrifuged, separated and distilled, and the lab results are crystal clear. When you go within, you begin to see the ego defenses, the sadness, the happiness, the light, the dark, the real you...the authentic self. Here, the trick is to feel, not think about how you feel. Surrender is a prerequisite for deep relaxation. You must surrender control, ego, competitiveness, time, results and simply let go. Relaxation cannot be forced. You cannot be fully present and mindful if you think, "I need to hurry up and meditate so I can do the laundry and return phone calls." The key to meditation and deep relaxation is letting go. We have to give ourselves permission to relax and find a place to recharge our batteries. To quiet your mind and feed your soul, create a peaceful spot in your home, perhaps an empty room or clutter-free space. Just the sight of a sparsely decorated room will help you feel lighter, freer and less cluttered mentally.

What happens to your body/mind during meditation? One of the many benefits is the slowing down of your thoughts. Researchers have shown heart rate, respiration, blood pressure and pulse all decrease with meditation and relaxation. Alpha brain waves, the brain waves associated with deep relaxation, increase in intensity and frequency. Blood lactate, a chemical associated with anxiety, has been found to fall rapidly within the first ten minutes of meditation. Several studies have shown people with definite hypertension can reduce their blood pressure after committing themselves to a regular routine of meditation, morning and night. Case in point: one of my meditation students had high blood pressure and began to practice deep breathing and meditation every morning for a minimum of twenty minutes. Tom was focused and determined to naturally lower his blood pressure so he would not be on medication for the rest of his life. After three months, his blood pressure decreased significantly - and his golf game improved dramatically! Meditation can do more than just relax you. It can create order out of chaos and soothe the turbulent waters of our inner seas. Meditation allows you to draw on a deep reservoir of peace and, when practiced daily, can be employed at a moment's notice.

Many of you probably meditate all the time and don't even know it. It is a bit like daydreaming but with much greater clarity and focus. Like daydreaming, you can employ your creativity to create an inner painting of what you desire. Guided imagery is a great tool for self-transformation and is akin to meditation. It is guided with the use of nature themes or healing themes and tends to be more structured than simple contemplation on a topic. One can combine the two themes to create guided meditations with imagery. Examples of guided meditations with imagery are found on the following pages and include "opening the heart" and "affirmations for wellness." It is very helpful to create a visual image in your mind's eye to deepen your connection with your inner canvas.

## Deep Breathing

Breath is the bridge between the body and the mind. It is the key to meditation. To deeply relax and meditate we first have to focus on our breathing. To live fully we must breathe fully. Most of us have become shallow breathers. Often our attitudes are reflected in our breathing. For example, if we feel tired, our breath tends to be shallow, a complacent inhale that says, "It is too much effort, I can't do everything." On the contrary, if we feel motivated, a deep inhale reflects our passion for life and inspires us to breathe with enthusiasm. The primary purpose of our breath is not simply to keep us alive but to move energy through the body via our breathing. By focusing on our breath, we create a flow of energy and awareness throughout, bathing every cell, tissue and organ with this dynamic energy.

Breathing is the subject of many books, spiritual practices, exercises and health reports. The reason for this emphasis underscores its importance in understanding the depth of transformation both physically and psychologically. The effects of certain types of breathing flabbergast me. For example, in Kundalini yoga, a form of breathing called breath of fire involves rapid inhalations and exhalations. It is designed to oxygenate and energize the body, increase blood flow, and clear the mind. Breathing is a powerful tool and can be used in a variety of ways to create different states of consciousness.

Deep, diaphragmatic breathing promotes relaxation and release. Notice how infants breathe; they take deep, diaphragmatic breaths...so should we. By fully expanding the lower lobes of our lungs, we allow more oxygen to flow through the body, especially to the brain. The brain consumes more than 20 percent of the body's oxygen, which is vital to clear thinking and memory recall. Deep breathing allows the central nervous system to relax, resulting in fewer stress hormones being released. Our inner system gets the message that it is now time for a peace break.

Begin to focus on your breathing by deeply inhaling and exhaling. Notice if there is any tension or tightness in your chest or abdomen. Feel the flow of oxygen moving down your lungs and expanding across your entire chest. Now begin to drop your shoulders down and consciously tell your whole body to relax. Uncross your legs; allow your whole body to become limp, soft and pliable as you read these words. This is how you meditate; you begin by focusing on your breathing, allowing your whole body/mind system to relax and then you go within and simply be.

In the following two chapters you will find guided meditations to aid you on your journey to peace and tranquility. An audio version of these guided meditations is found on side two of the cassette tape, listed on the order form on page 135.

CHAPTER 33

# Affirmations for Wellness
# (Guided Meditation)

*F*ind a quiet, peaceful space where you will not be disturbed. Either sit or lie down, whichever is more comfortable for you. Allow your body to become completely relaxed. Then gently go within.

Focus on the flow of your breath, easily inhaling and exhaling. Center your mind and allow the body to surrender into a state of total relaxation.

With the body relaxed and the mind at ease, visualize yourself as the beautiful well being that you are. Remind yourself that you are beautiful just the way you are. Allow your body, mind and spirit to deeply feel the following affirmations:

- I am the embodiment of wellness.
- I am light.
- I am radiant.
- I am peace.
- Everyday in every way I am getting better and better.
- Each moment I continue to grow and glow.
- My immune system functions at an optimal level.
- I am healthy.
- I am whole.
- I am strong.
- I am vibrant.
- I am light and loving with everyone I meet.
- I am intelligent, gifted and talented
- I am the creator of my own reality.
- I am the conscious, joyful creator of my experiences.
- I am empowered.

> "Affirmation of life is the spiritual act by which man ceases to live unreflectively and begins to devote himself to his life with reverence in order to raise it to its true value. To affirm life is to deepen, to make more inward, and to exalt the will to live."
>
> ALBERT SCHWEITZER

127

- ◆ I am the source of my own joy and peace.
- ◆ I am in control of my emotions and feelings.
- ◆ I speak from my heart.
- ◆ I allow everyone to be who they are.
- ◆ I live by love and unconditionally love myself and others.
- ◆ I am free to be who I truly am.
- ◆ Every cell, tissue and organ in my body works in perfect concert to create a symphony of sound health.
- ◆ I believe love is all that matters.
- ◆ I believe love is the most powerful healer in the universe and each of us comes fully equipped to love.
- ◆ Health is my natural state of being.
- ◆ I am thankful for each new day and grateful for all the people, things, opportunities and events in my life.
- ◆ I believe everything is a stepping stone along my path of growth and evolution.
- ◆ I believe the basis of my life is freedom, the objective of my life is love and joy and the result of my life is growth.
- ◆ I am constantly growing, evolving and creating a wonderful, well version of myself.
- ◆ I do not have to prove myself worthy to anyone or anything.
- ◆ I am worthy to give and receive love because I am worthy.
- ◆ I am a peaceful, powerful soul.
- ◆ I know no one or nothing can affect me unless I let them.
- ◆ I believe I honor myself by having self-respect.
- ◆ I love myself unconditionally.
- ◆ I feel love is all there is.
- ◆ I believe health and well-being are my birthright.
- ◆ I affirm all is well, everything is working out for my highest good and I am safe.

Allow these powerful affirmations to be absorbed by your body, mind and spirit. Know that these thoughts are working! Know in your heart of hearts that belief becomes biology, so believe in your optimal wellness and know you are a magnificent, well being. Wellness is only a thought away.

Now gently bring your awareness back to your breathing, slowly inhaling and exhaling. Re-emerge refreshed, rejuvenated and totally at peace.

# CHAPTER 34

# OPENING THE HEART
# (Guided Meditation)

$T$ake a deep breath and allow yourself to be in the present moment. For this moment in time, forget about the past, forget about the future and simply be still in the moment. This now moment is ripe with possibility.

Focus on your breathing, deeply inhaling and exhaling. Now gently bring your attention to your chest. Begin to breathe deeply into the lower lobes of your lungs and feel the expansion of your entire chest cavity.

Notice if there is any tension or tightness in the chest or heart area and simply breathe away the tension by paying attention to the tension. Breathing into the heart allows for the opening of the heart chakra, an energy center vital to your overall well-being. From these energy centers, the life force flows through the physical body, restoring and cleansing it. When the free flow of energy or life force is impeded or blocked, diseases can result. The heart is filled with both pain and joy so we are consciously going to open the heart and allow the pain from the past to be safely released.

Allow your attention to turn to your heart center once again...picture a beautiful pink flower bud bursting with potential. It is almost ready to bloom but requires some attention to prepare it for its full blossoming. With each breath, visualize and allow all the tension, pain, disappointment, sadness and fear to float away from you and feel the light pouring into you.

Go deeper still and allow yourself to heal the wounded child that thinks she is less than she is. Allow the latent images to emerge. Extract the essence of those painful lessons and integrate them into your greater knowingness.

With each breath, feel the tension in your chest dissipating and appreciate the feeling of lightness re-emerging. Remove self-limiting thoughts that keep you from your brilliance and consciously give yourself permission to let your light shine.

Now turn your attention to the flower. Notice how the bud has now become a beautiful, fragrant pink rose sparkling with the love you feel for yourself. The heart is all about love and when the heart is open, we are open to give and receive this magical elixir of love. Smile into the knowingness that you have an infinite capacity to love.

Breathe in this love and light and feel it spread throughout your whole body in waves of love. Feel as though you are now in an ocean of love being gently caressed by radiant waves of love and light. Notice how these beautiful waves of love have a pink irides-cent color that further soothes your soul. Smile into the knowing-ness that love is all there is. Open your heart to increase your capac-ity to give and receive love.

Having cleansed the heart and bathed the entire area with love and light, visualize a protective, permeable shield around your heart so that only good comes to you and only good comes from you.

Your heart is now open and the wounds are healing. Make a conscious effort to keep your heart open and allow your love and light to shine through. Let each day be an outpouring of love and light as you grow and evolve. See the light of your love healing yourself and all those you come in contact with.

Open your heart to a whole new way of loving, and re-emerge refreshed, whole and full of love.

# CHAPTER 35

# Epilogue: You, The Self Master

*I* believe we are on the precipice of a bright new future, an age of peace and non-violence. The most important part of this new era is you. You are the conscious creator of your own reality. Now is the time to purposefully create the perfect reality based on your own desires and deeper heartfelt truths. This special time is a wonderful opportunity to crystallize your vision. Go within and ask your heart what brings you the greatest joy. As was so eloquently stated in *Conversations with God, An Uncommon Dialogue, Book 1*, by Neale Donald Walsch, "Be the greatest version of the grandest vision you have ever held about who you really are."

We are at a special point in history, a "zero point" where we must consciously relinquish the past, the future and any and all beliefs that limit our pure potential. We must say goodbye to endless years of human history tainted by wars, poverty, racial intolerance, fear, separation and misplaced material focus. We must consciously co-create a world of peace, justice, harmony, service, tolerance, acceptance and reverence for Earth and all its inhabitants. As we co-create this new age, we must be proactive and not passive – it is time to take action and make the world a better place for all. We can no longer operate in isolation or egocentric ways, for there is a greater truth unfolding. We are beginning to realize that we are all one; when one of us hurts, all of us hurt, and when one of us heals, all of us heal. Small actions performed by many make a big difference.

Don't think you can't make a difference; you can and you will. Just by contributing positive thoughts you make the world a better place. Simply by choosing to not judge someone because they believe differently than you goes a long way toward creating a culture of acceptance and non-judgment. Believe in your power to make the world a better place and take your emergency brake off! Let your light shine and be passionate about the betterment of your world. We are powerful, bright, intelligent creators who have choices to make. So choose to be well, choose to allow others to be

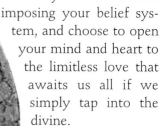

The Ages of Man

who they are without imposing your belief system, and choose to open your mind and heart to the limitless love that awaits us all if we simply tap into the divine.

Make this moment and all others a celebration of life, of love, of laughter and joy. Practice the art of non-violence in your thoughts, words and actions. Be mindful of thoughts that hurt yourself or others and act from a place of peace and self-respect. There is only one person in the world who can make you happy and that is you, the self master. There is only one person in the world that can make you unhappy and that is you, the unawakened. See the world with new eyes, eyes filled with compassion for the smallest among us as well as the seemingly misled. Allow your thoughts to lift and bless those around you. If each of us were at peace with ourselves, there would be world peace. One of the best ways to heal the planet is to heal yourself. *Focus on becoming the master within.* I invite you to be the conscious creators of the new millennium and the new you. May love and light make each day of your life sparkle like the diamond you are.

> *"We shall not cease from exploration
> And the end of all our exploring
> Will be to arrive where we started
> And know the place for the first time"*
>
> T.S. ELIOT

# References and Recommended Readings

Ader, R., *Psychoneuroimmunology,* 2nd Ed. Academic Press, San Diego. 1991.

Bailey, C., *The New Fit or Fat.* Houghton Mifflin, Boston. 1991

Barker, J., *Future Edge.* William Morrow Co., New York. 1992

Benson, H., *Timeless Healing: The Power and Biology of Belief.* Scribner, New York. 1996

Borysenko, F. and M., *Minding the Body, Mending the Mind.* Hay House, Calif. 1987

Buscaglia, L., *Born to Love.* Fawcettt Crest, New York. 1972

Capra, F., *The Tao of Physics.* Shambhala, Boston. 1991

Chopra, D., *Ageless Body, Timeless Mind: The Quantum Alternative to Growing Old.* Harmony, New York. 1993

Cook, R., (Ed.), *One Hundred and One Famous Poems.* Contemporary Books, Chicago. 1958

Cousins, N., *Head First: The Biology of Hope.* Penguin Books, New York. 1989

Czimbal, B., Zadikov, M., *Vitamin T, A Guide to Healthy Touch.* Open Book, Oregon. 1991

Dossey, L., *Healing Words: The Power of Prayer and the Practice of Medicine.* Harper Collins, New York. 1993

Dychtwald, K., *BODYMIND.* Penguin Putnam Inc., New York. 1977

Feng, G., & English, J., *Lao Tsu, Tao Te Ching.* Random House, New York. 1972

Fisher, I. (Ed.), *The Essential Gandhi, An Anthology of His Writings on His Life and His Ideas.* Random House, New York. 1962

Fox, M., *The Reinvention of Work: A New Vision of Livelihood for Our Time.* Harper Collins Publishers, New York. 1994

Gibran, K., *The Prophet,* Alfred A. Knopf, New York. 1981

Hanh, T., *Peace is Every Step,* Bantam Books, New York. 1992

Hay, L., *You Can Heal Your Life.* Hay House, Calif. 1984

Hendricks, G. & K., *Conscious Loving*. Bantam Books, New York. 1992

Hirshfield, J., (Ed.), *Women in Praise of the Sacred, 43 Centuries of Spiritual Poetry by Women*. Harper Collins Publishers, New York. 1994

Jung, C., *Man and His Symbols*. Dell Publishing Co., New York. 1964

Kabat-Zinn, J., *Full Catastrophe Living*. Delacorte Press, New York. 1990

LeDoux, J., *The Emotional Brain*. Simon & Schuster, New York. 1996

McWilliams, P., *The LIFE 101 Quote Book*. Prelude Press, CA. 1996

Mehrabian, A., *Silent Messages: Implicit Communication of Emotions and Attitudes, 2nd Edition*. Wadworth Publishing Co., New York. 1981

Pelletier, K., *Mind as Healer, Mind as Slayer*. Dell Publishing, New York. 1977/1992

Pennebaker, J., *Opening Up: The Healing Power of Confiding in Others*. William Morrow & Co., New York. 1990

Pert, C., *Molecules of Emotion*. Scribner, New York. 1997

Rechellbacher, H., *Aveda Rituals*. Henry Holt and Company, LLC, New York. 1999.

Seligman, M., *Learned Optimism*. Knopf, New York. 1990

Senge, P., *The Fifth Discipline: The Art and Practice of a Learning Organization*. Doubleday, New York. 1990

Tunis, E., *Indians*. The World Publishing Co., Ohio. 1959

Walsch, N., *Conversations with God, An Uncommon Dialogue, Books 1, 2 & 3*. Hampton Roads Publishing Co., VA. 1996

Weil, A., *Natural Health, Natural Medicine*. Houghton Millflin, Boston. 1995

Williamson, M., *Return to Love*. Harper Collins, New York. 1992

Yogananda, P., *Autobiography of a Yogi*. Self Realization Fellowship, Los Angeles. 1969

To buy additional copies of *Exploratory Surgery of the Soul, A Journey to Self Mastery* or other resources from Self Mastery International, feel free to photocopy the order form below.

## ORDER FORM

## Four convenient ways to order:

By phone/fax: Call 1-828-863-4681

By mail:    Self Mastery International
373 Landrum Rd.
Tryon, NC 28782

By e-mail: pfarmer@teleplex.net

By website: www.selfmasteryintl.com

Please send me:

_____  Copies of Exploratory Surgery of the Soul @ $18.00 each

_____  Copies of Exploratory Surgery of the Soul audio cassette @ $10.00 each

_____  Copies of Inner Awakenings video @ $20.00 each

Name: _____

Address: _____

City/State/Zip: _____

Daytime Phone: _____

**Shipping:** $4.00 for first item and $2.00 for each additional item.
**Payment Method:** ☐ Check ☐ Visa ☐ MasterCard

Card Number : _____

Name on card: _____ Exp. Date    / \_\_\_\_\_

# Self Mastery Seminars/Keynotes and Other Services:

Self Mastery International is committed to assisting individuals and companies achieve self mastery through various programs, seminars, keynotes, retreats and resources. A sampling of some of the keynotes and seminars recently showcased by Dr. Peggy Farmer are:

- The New Millennium, The New You
- The Well Woman
- The ABC's of Self Mastery
- Finding Purpose in Your Life and Passion in Your Work
- Leading from the Heart
- The Art of Managing Stress Before It Manages You
- The Art of Compassionate, Effective Communication
- Emotional Intelligence…A Tool for the Future
- EQ Mapping and the Business Case for Emotional Intelligence
- From Conflict to Resolution
- The Art of Managing Time
- TEAM, Together Each Achieves More
- Wellness in the Workplace

Dr. Farmer routinely hosts weekend retreats that allow participants to experience in-depth exercises and soulful self-discovery. Some of the retreats include:

- Adventures of the Heart (couples retreat)
- Rekindling the Feminine Fire (women's wellness retreat)
- Beyond the Mother/Daughter Connection (mother/daughter retreat)
- TEAM (corporate team building retreat)
- The Road to Wellness, A Woman's Journey to Wholeness (women's wellness retreat)

If you are interested in any of the above programs or would like a tailor-made program for you or your organization, contact us by phone at:

Self Mastery International, 1-828-863-4681
or email us at pfarmer@teleplex.net.
Our website is www.selfmasteryintl.com